Countryknits

Countryknits

Complete patterns and instructions
for 23 casual sweaters
inspired by American folk designs

Carol Huber

E. P. Dutton   New York

Book design by Marilyn Rey

CONTENTS

INTRODUCTION

It's easy to see why America loves Americana. Freshness, versatility, and naïvete all blend into beautiful and original designs and patterns that have been cherished, used over and over, and handed down from generation to generation. Many contemporary motifs can be traced back to the 18th century and textile decoration, in particular, shows an unbroken connection from America's earliest days to the present. Quilt patterns from the 18th and 19th centuries are still being used, samplers are copied, plaid and check blankets are created in the identical weaves of centuries past. These are heirloom patterns, and yet they are so comfortably appropriate for today's lifestyle.

My husband and I are antiques dealers specializing in textiles, and we are fortunate enough to come in contact with many exquisite, museum-quality pieces. Looking at these wonderful objects—bedcovers, hearth rugs, embroidered pockets, samplers, needlework pictures, to name a few—we decided that many of the designs used could be successfully transformed into sweater patterns. Having been a textile major in college, I began graphing a few so that they could be knit locally. (I immediately discovered that I could design much faster than I could knit, and I was so excited about the project that as soon as I had one pattern off the drawing board I would begin another.) The response was great! Everyone loved these "folky" sweaters, and we soon found ourselves hiring knitters to make them up for friends and people that had heard about them by word of mouth. Soon our orders for sweaters were heavier than the local knitters could handle and this led to trips to England where we set up networks of knitters to fill our Stateside orders.

Not everyone, however, wanted a completed sweater, and we soon had requests from knitters who wanted to do their own knitting. We began packaging a few of our designs in kit form, but soon found that knitters wanted all of the patterns; thus the demand and enthusiasm from these early knitters was the inspiration for this book.

The patterns and directions are different from those found in most knitting books. The directions are easy to follow, and they show you how to substitute yarns, to make size adjustments, and to make your own adaptations. The formulas are easy and can be adapted to all of your other knitting projects. Our patterns are colorful, casual, and comfortable—Americana at its best! You'll discover that our Sampler design was created from a Balch School sampler wrought in Rhode Island in the 18th century. Some of the checks and plaids will probably look familiar, for they were inspired by the great textiles made by the Shakers. Quilt patterns have worked into wonderful adaptations: the Irish Chain is a delightful variation on the run-of-the-mill argyle design; the Basket pattern makes a sprightly sweater; and the Log Cabin and Bargello designs are very handsome graphics.

We think you'll like all of these patterns, will enjoy knitting them in a vast array of yarns, and will find that your sweaters will become a tradition, just as the designs which inspired them are!

KNITTING NOTES

ABBREVIATIONS:

alt	alternate
beg	begin(ning)
cont	continue
dec	decrease
inc	increase
K	knit
P	purl
st	stitch
st st	stockinette stitch
tog	together

TENSION OR GAUGE:

These terms are often used interchangeably. They refer to how tightly or how loosely the knitter is knitting compared with the gauge given in the pattern or by the yarn manufacturer. The gauge is the number of stitches *and* the number of rows to equal one inch. It is very important in knitting to keep this gauge correct as a mistake is multiplied with each row and the pattern will become either elongated or compressed. The horizontal gauge is the number of stitches to make one inch and determines the finished chest size. The vertical gauge is the number of rows to equal one inch and determines the finished length.

Knit a tension square before you begin any garment. Work a 2-inch square in stockinette stitch. Lay it flat and carefully measure the rows and stitches to equal one inch in each direction. If your work is larger than the specified gauge your tension is too loose and you should move down to a smaller needle. If your measurement comes out smaller, your tension is too tight and you should move to a larger needle.

DETERMINING AND ALTERING SIZE:

To determine the size garment to knit, take a chest measurement and add 2 to 4 inches depending on how tight or how loose you want the sweater to fit. (Remember, wool tends to stretch a bit.) Compare your tension with the gauge and make any needle corrections. Take measurements for the following: length of finished garment from underarm, length of finished garment from middle of shoulder, and length of finished sleeve to underarm. Compare your measurements with those given for the pattern and lengthen or shorten as needed.

SIZING:

(1) Measure chest. (2) Add 2 to 4 inches (depending on how loose you want the sweater). (3) Divide total measurement by 2. (4) Multiply this number by the number of sts in one inch. This gives the number of sts needed for front and back. (5) Subtract 8 from above number for ribbing. (6) Cast on number of sts from step 5. Work in ribbing for K1, P1 for 3 inches and increase 8 sts in next row using st st. (7) Follow graph, deleting or adding pattern from graph at sides. Work to underarm. (8) Measure from underarm to desired length. (9) Subtract 3 inches (ribbing). (10) Multiply by number of rows per inch. This gives the number of rows for desired underarm length. (11) Adjust graph by adding or deleting as necessary. (12) Measure desired length to neck edge of shoulder. (13) Subtract underarm length. (14) Multiply by the number of rows per inch. This gives the number of rows for desired length from underarm to shoulder. (Allow a little extra for sufficient arm movement.) (15) Unless you are knitting a very large (over 44″), or very small (under 34″) garment, the neck will not need

adjustment. However, sts can be added or deleted and neck edge moved in or out. (16) Shoulders will have the number of sts determined by the number cast on at beginning. At underarm bind off according to chart and follow decreasing. (17) At shoulder divide total number of sts on each side by 3. Bind off as pattern shows. (18) Measure length of sleeve to underarm. (19) Subtract 3 inches for ribbing. (20) Multiply by the number of rows per inch. Adjust pattern by adding or deleting rows. (21) Follow pattern for top of shoulder. (22) For small sizes (34 and under) delete 2 to 3 sts each side of sleeve pattern. For large sizes (44 and over) add 2 to 3 sts each side of sleeve pattern.

An alternative method of adjusting the size is to increase the size of the garment by using bulkier yarns or to decrease the size of the sweater by using finer yarns. The yarn-gauge chart shows many different yarns, a needle number, and the number of stitches per inch and the number of rows per inch. Check your gauge with the graph to determine the size garment you will end up with by following the charted graph with a different yarn.

GRAPHS:

The patterns in this book are all charted on graphs. Each square represents one stitch. The patterns are shown in color, or in black and white. The black-and-white have different symbols to distinguish the colors. Adjustments can be made by adding or deleting rows, or moving the side seam and armhole line in or out. Increase and decrease stitches are indicated on the sides, and binding off is designated by decreasing more than one stitch.

ADAPTING PATTERNS TO DIFFERENT SWEATERS:

Many of the patterns in this book lend themselves to more than one sweater shape. The Country Goose crewneck pullover, for example, is also shown as a cardigan. Other designs can be changed by using the outline from one sweater and the design graph from another. Cardigan possibilities include: Tree-of-Life, Irish Chain, Double Irish Chain, Flying Geese, Bargello, Log Cabin, Strawberry, Diamonds, Patchwork Sampler, and Windowpane. V-neck vests or pullovers suggested are: Irish Chain, Double Irish Chain, Flying Geese, Shaker Blanket, Diamonds, Plaid Blanket, Old Rectory, and Windowpane. Possibilities are endless by using combinations of patterns and different yarns.

YARN-GAUGE CHARTS:

The yarn-gauge charts are included so that one can quickly convert a pattern from one type of yarn to another. Heavy-weight wools can be used for sweaters calling for sport-weight yarn, or vice versa, by adjusting the pattern according to the above directions and using the yarn-gauge charts as a guide to needle size and tension. It's fun; by all means experiment!

KNITTING THE GARMENT:

Here are a few general notes on the actual knitting of the sweater. For a neater edge, whenever possible slip the first stitch and knit into the back of the last stitch on every row. This will create a neater edge, and it will be easier to sew and match up the pattern.

Do not join yarn in the middle of a row; it usually shows and creates a bulky area. Join at the beginning of the row with a new ball and use both ends for sewing seams later.

An especially important note about the sweater patterns in this book. Do not carry the yarn across the back of the sweater when working pattern motifs. Use bobbins (or small balls) and change yarn with each color change simply by looping the first yarn around the new color and continuing with the new yarn. This is very important with heavy yarns as they tend to pucker and become bulky.

SEWING TOGETHER:

To join the garment together, use the same yarn it was knitted with. Use a running stitch and go through each stitch on each side of the seam. (A back stitch makes the seam bulky, and an overcast stitch is not as neat.) Make sure not to pull the yarn too tightly and secure the ends of the seam with a double stitch. Weave in all ends two or three inches before cutting. Do not knot sewing yarns.

BLOCKING:

Wool and cotton sweaters should be pressed when completed so that the seams will lie flat. When blocking, use a damp cloth and a warm iron. Lay the seams flat and press down with the iron but do not go back and forth. Wool tends to mat and become shiny if pressed too long. It is easier to sew the shoulder and sleeve/armhole seams first and then press before sewing the long sleeve and side seam.

WASHING:

Hand-knitted garments should be hand-washed. Use a mild detergent and lukewarm water. Do not rub, wring, twist, scrub, or let the water run directly on the garment. Gently push the sweater into the water and lightly agitate it up and down. Do not soak for long as this mats wool. Rinse thoroughly, squeeze slightly, and roll between two towels to remove excess water. Lay flat and smooth back into shape.

YARN-GAUGE CHART

Group A Yarns	Needle Size	Gauge
George Picaud Lambswool	5	7 sts 8½ rows
Columbia-Minerva Scotch Fingering	4	7 sts 9 rows
Columbia-Minerva Nantuck Fingering	4	7 sts 9 rows

Group B Yarns	Needle Size	Gauge
Columbia-Minerva Featherweight Knitting Worsted	5	6 sts 7½ rows
Columbia-Minerva Shetland Wool	5	6 sts 7½ rows
Bernat Berella Sportspun	5	6 sts 8 rows
Picaud Laine et Coton	5	6 sts 8 rows
Chat Botte Petrouchka	4	6 sts 8 rows
3 Suisses Suizy DK	5	6 sts 6½ rows
Patons Clansman DK	4	6½ sts 7½ rows
S. & C. Huber's American Classic 100% cotton	5	6 sts 6½ rows

Group C Yarns	Needle Size	Gauge
S. & C. Huber's American Classic 100% wool, Fisherman 2-ply	6	5 sts 6½ rows
Galler's Olympic-Supra 100% wool	8	5 sts 6 rows
Unger Natuurwol	6	5 sts 6 rows
Pingouin Comfortable Sport	6	5 sts 6½ rows
Galler's Cotton Express	6	5 sts 6 rows
Galler's Parisian Cotton RBC	6	5 sts 6 rows
Columbia-Minerva Nantuck Sports	6	5 sts 7 rows
Bernat Sesame 4	8	5 sts 7 rows
Bernat Berella "4"	8	5 sts 7 rows
Galler's Pony, 100% cotton	5	5½ sts 6½ rows
Unger's Britania	6	5½ sts 7 rows
Lister-Lee Motoravia DK	5	5½ sts 8 rows
Phildar Sagittaire	4	5½ sts 8 rows

Group D Yarns	Needle Size	Gauge
Sunbeam Aran	7	4½ sts 6 rows
Columbia-Minerva Knitting Worsted	8	4½ sts 6 rows
Columbia-Minerva Heatherglo	8	4½ sts 6 rows
Nantuck 4-ply Knitting Worsted	8	4½ sts 6 rows
Nantuck Dimension	8	4½ sts 6 rows
Nantuck Spectra	8	4½ sts 6 rows
Reverie	8	4½ sts 6 rows

SIZE CHART

(Number of stitches needed for the front or the back)

Finished Size	34	36	38	40	42	44
Group A Yarns	119	126	133	140	147	154
Group B Yarns	102	108	114	120	126	132
Group C Yarns	85	90	95	100	105	110
Group D Yarns	76	81	86	90	94	99

NEEDLE CONVERSION CHART

Metric U.K. & Australia	U.K., Australia Canada, S. Africa	U.S.A.
2	14	00
2¼	13	0
2¾	12	1
3	11	2
3¼	10	3
3¾	9	4
4	8	5
4½	7	6
5	6	7
5½	5	8
6	4	9
6½	3	10
7	2	10½
7½	1	11
8	0	12
9	00	13
10	000	15

Country Goose Crew-Neck Pullover

COUNTRY GOOSE CREW-NECK PULLOVER

Our whimsical Goose sweater combines a whole array of folk art motifs: hearts, flowers, checks, stripes, and geese. A colorful band design on an off-white ground, with red, navy, light blue, dark green, light green, yellow, brown, and gold. It makes up into a charming country sweater.

MATERIALS: 14 oz. off-white or other background color in knitting worsted. 3 oz. of dark green, light blue, and light green. 2 oz. of red and dark blue. 1 oz. of yellow, gold, and dark brown.

NEEDLES: Size 4 and 7. One set of double-point needles, size 4.

GAUGE: 5 sts. = 1 inch, 6½ rows = 1 inch using knitting worsted.

SIZE: These directions are for a size 38″ finished garment. Measurements are as follows: length to underarm 15¾″, length to shoulder 25″, length of sleeve to underarm 18″.

To alter size see instructions for SIZING.

FRONT: With size 4 needles, cast on 80 sts. Work in K1, P1, ribbing for 3 inches. Change to size 7 needles and increase 8 sts evenly spaced on next row, working in st st. Continue in st st and work the charted design, binding off and decreasing as indicated. Place 14 sts in center of front on holder to be picked up for neck later.

BACK: Work back to match front using chart for pattern. Fill in pattern at neck with designs being used and place 26 sts in center of back on holder for neck ribbing later.

SLEEVES: Cast on 40 sts on size 4 needles and work in ribbing K1, P1, for 3 inches. Change to size 7 needles and increase 8 sts evenly spaced in next row using st st. Work sleeves according to charted design.

Sew shoulder seams.

NECK: With size 4 double-point needles, K across sts on back holder with right side facing. Pick up and K 56 sts to right shoulder (including sts on front holder). K1, P1, in ribbing on 80 sts for 1 inch. Bind off loosely in ribbing.

Sew sleeves in place. Sew underarm and sleeve seams. Weave in loose threads. Block lightly with damp cloth and warm iron.

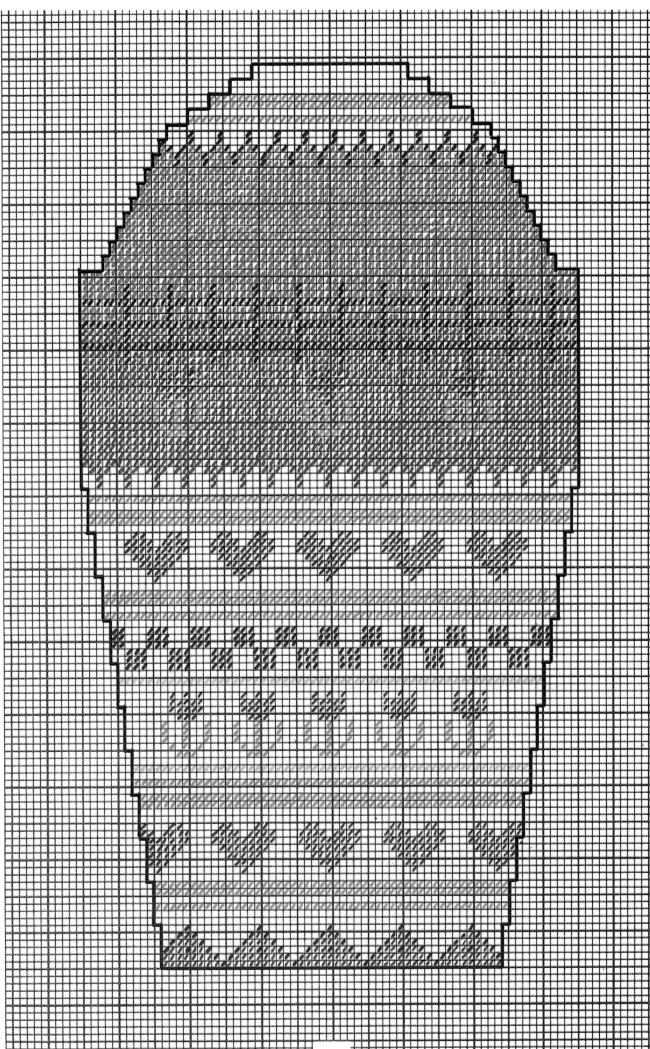

COUNTRY GOOSE CARDIGAN

Use the basic instructions for the Country Goose Pullover and work the front as follows:

LEFT FRONT: With size 4 needles cast on 37 sts. Work in K1, P1, ribbing for 3 inches. Change to size 7 needles and increase 3 sts evenly spaced on next row using st st. Continue in st st working pattern according to charted design. Sts at center front of neck are to be placed on a holder for neck band.

RIGHT FRONT: Work as left front, but using chart for right front.

BACK: Work same as back for pullover.

SLEEVES: Work same as sleeves for pullover.

BUTTONHOLE BAND: Cast on 11 sts with size 4 needles. Work 4 rows K1, P1, ribbing.
Next row: K1, P1, twice. Cast off 3 sts. K1, P1 twice.
Next row: K1, P1, twice. Cast on 3 sts. K1, P1 twice.
Work 18 rows in K1, P1 ribbing.
Continue as above until 7 buttonholes in all have been worked.
Rib 16 more rows. Place sts on holder.

Work band for other side omitting buttonholes.

Sew buttonhole band to right front and plain band to left front.
Sew shoulder seams.

NECKBAND: Work with right side facing. Rib across sts on buttonhole band using size 4 needles. Pick up and K sts on holder from right front neck, across sts from back holder, across sts from left front and left band (107 sts).
Rib one row.
2nd and 3rd rows: Buttonhole as before.
Work 4 more rows in K1, P1 ribbing.
Bind off in ribbing.

Sew sleeves in place. Sew underarm and sleeve seams. Weave in loose threads. Block lightly with damp cloth and warm iron.

Schoolhouse Crew-Neck Pullover

SCHOOLHOUSE CREW-NECK PULLOVER

A classic design taken from a 19th-century quilt pattern. This motif has been effectively used in pottery, stationery, tote bags, and boxes, to name just a few. It looks equally good in a sweater and works up quickly.

MATERIALS: 16 to 18 oz. of knitting worsted wool weight for background, 4 to 6 oz. of 2 contrasting colors.

NEEDLES: Size 4 and 7. One set of double-point needles, size 4.

GAUGE: 5 sts = 1 inch, 6½ rows = 1 inch.

SIZE: These directions are for a size 38″ finished garment. Measurements are as follows: length to underarm 15¾″, length to shoulder 25″, length of sleeve to underarm 18″.

To alter size see instructions for SIZING.

FRONT: With size 4 needles, cast on 80 sts. Work in K1, P1, ribbing for 3 inches. Change to size 7 needles and increase 8 sts evenly spaced on next row working in st st. Continue in st st and work the charted design, binding off and decreasing as indicated. Place the 14 sts in center of front on holder to be picked up later for neck ribbing.

BACK: Work back to match front. Fill in pattern at neck to shoulders and place 26 sts in center of back on holder for neck ribbing.

SLEEVES: Cast on 40 sts on size 4 needles. Work in K1, P1, ribbing for 3 inches. Change to size 7 needles and increase 8 sts evenly spaced in next row using st st. Work sleeves according to charted design.

Sew shoulder seams.

NECK: With size 4 double-point needles, K across sts on back holder with right side facing. Pick up and K 56 sts to right shoulder (including sts on front holder). K1, P1, in ribbing on 80 sts for 1 inch. Bind off loosely in ribbing.

Sew sleeves in place. Sew underarm and sleeve seams. Weave in loose threads. Block lightly with damp cloth and warm iron.

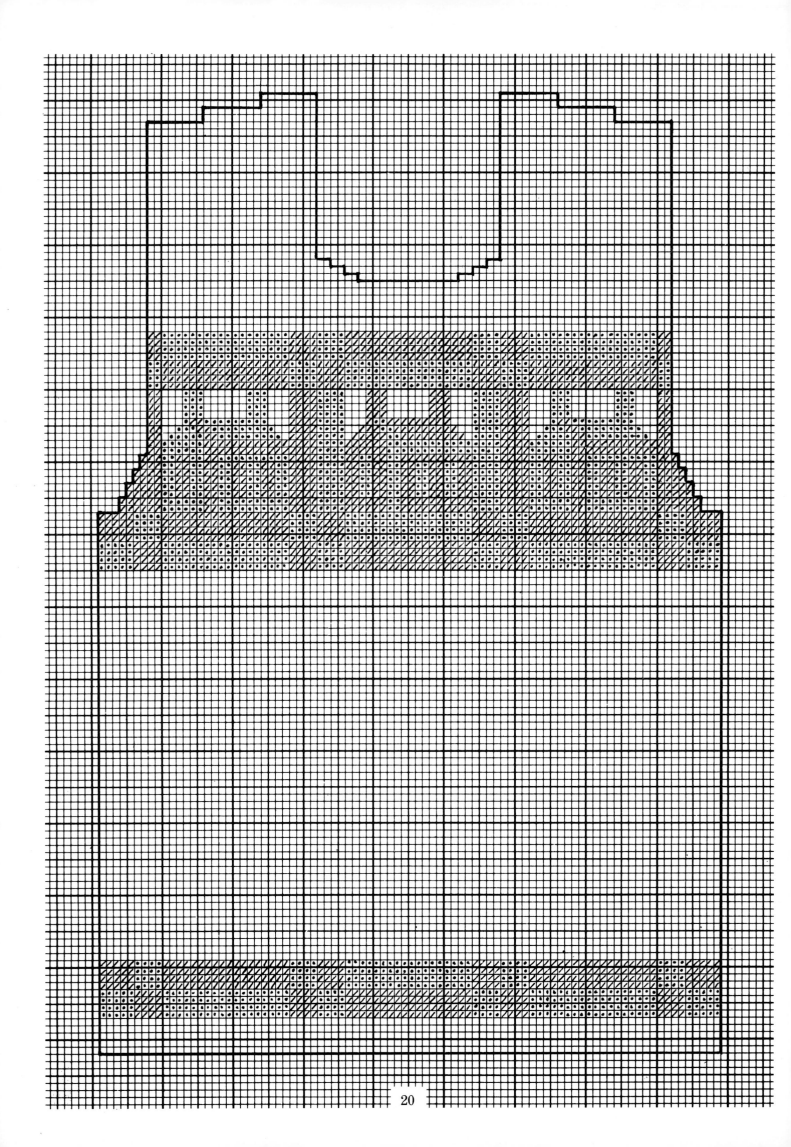

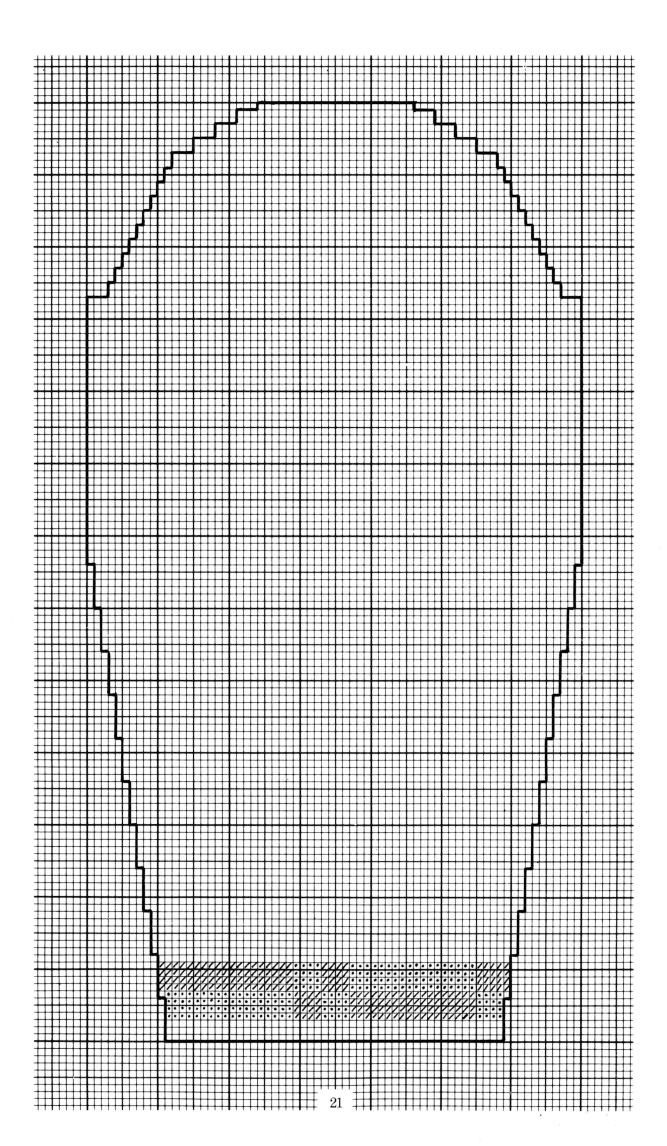

Irish Chain Crew-Neck Pullover

IRISH CHAIN CREW-NECK PULLOVER

Inspired by the popular 19th-century Irish Chain quilt pattern, this classic sweater is a great alternative to the ever-popular argyle and a wonderful addition to any wardrobe.

MATERIALS: 20 to 22 oz. main color and 6 to 8 oz. of contrasting color in knitting worsted wool weight.

NEEDLES: Size 4 and 7. One set of double-point needles, size 4.

GAUGE: 5 sts = 1 inch, 6½ rows = 1 inch.

SIZE: These directions are for a size 38″ finished garment. Measurements are as follows: length to underarm 16¾″, length to shoulder 26″, length of sleeve to underarm 18″.

To alter size see instructions for SIZING.

FRONT: With size 4 needles, cast on 80 sts. Work in K1, P1, ribbing for 3 inches. Change to size 7 needles and increase 8 sts evenly spaced on next row working in st st. Continue in st st and work the charted design, binding off and decreasing as indicated. Place the 14 sts in center of front on holder to be picked up later for neck ribbing.

BACK: Work back to match front using charted pattern. Fill in pattern at neck with correlating design and place 26 sts in center of back on holder for neck ribbing.

SLEEVES: Cast on 40 sts on size 4 needles. Work in K1, P1, ribbing for 3 inches. Change to size 7 needles and increase 8 sts evenly spaced in next row using st st. Work sleeves according to charted design.

Sew shoulder seams.

NECK: With size 4 double-point needles, K across sts on back holder with right side facing. Pick up and K 56 sts to right shoulder (including sts on front holder). K1, P1, in ribbing on 80 sts for 1 inch. Bind off loosely in ribbing.

Sew sleeves in place. Sew underarm and sleeve seams. Weave in loose threads. Block lightly with damp cloth and warm iron.

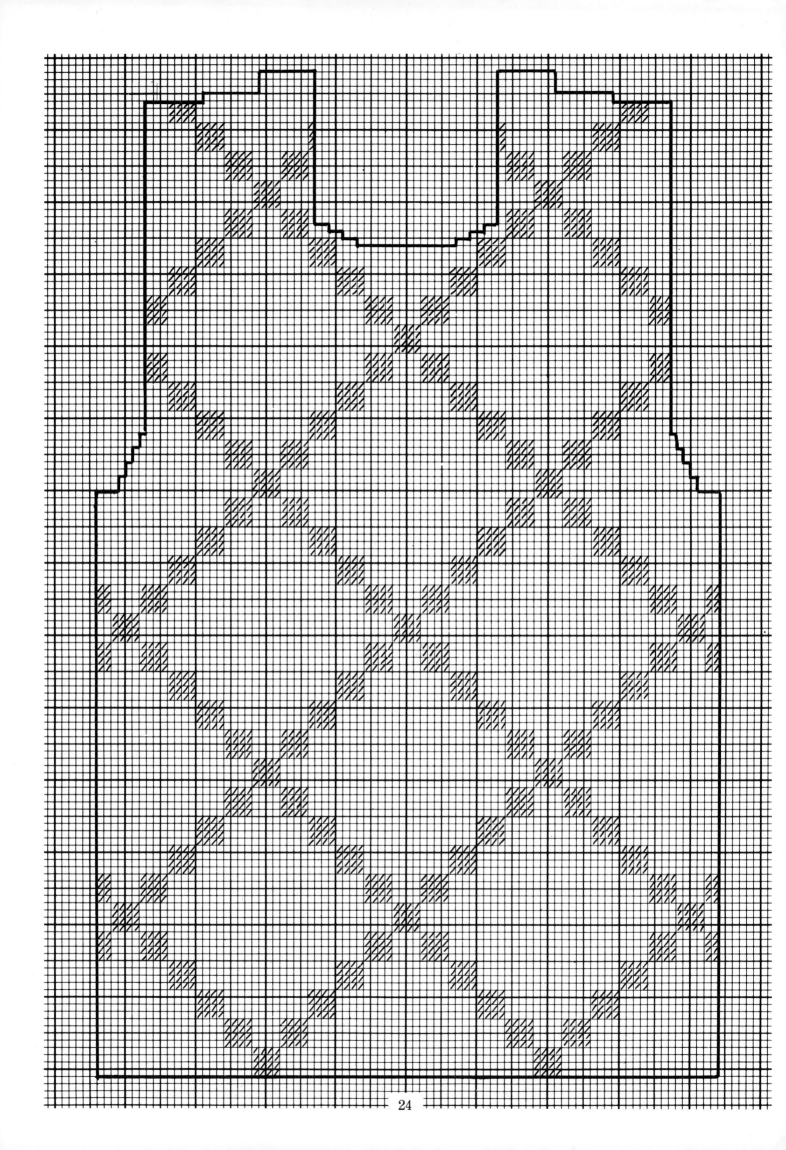

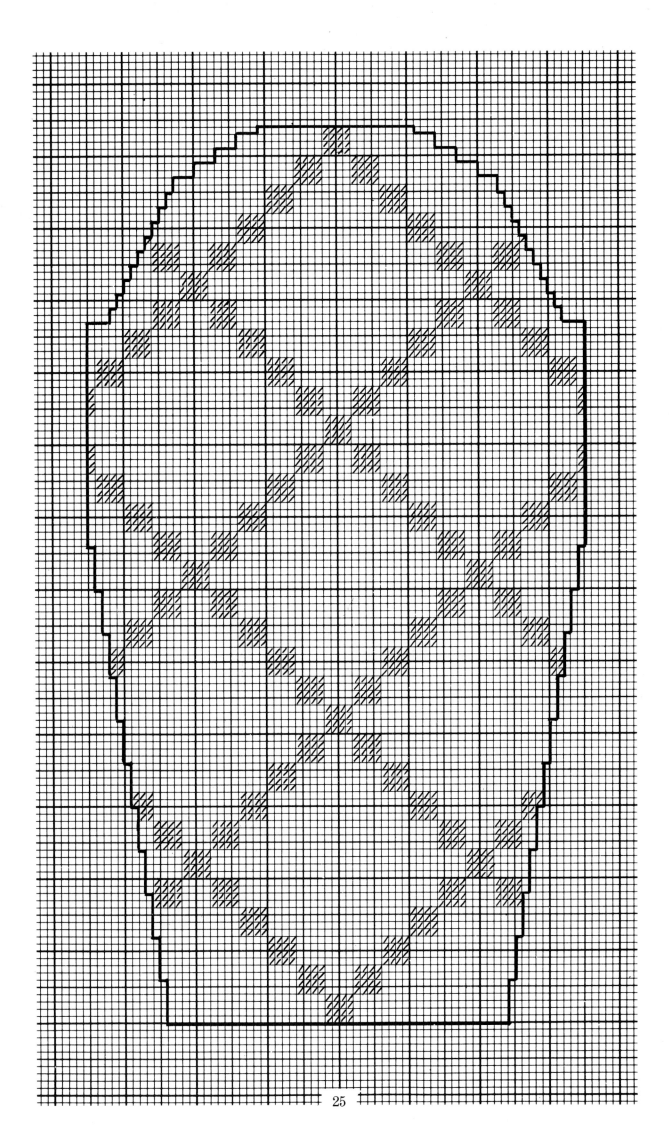

Sampler Crew-Neck Pullover

SAMPLER CREW-NECK PULLOVER

Samplers are one of the most decorative and visual forms of early needlework. They come in a variety of sizes and designs and were worked by girls as part of their education, sometimes at school, sometimes at home. This design is an adaptation of a "Balch School" sampler wrought in Rhode Island in the late 18th century.

MATERIALS: 20 to 22 oz. off-white or other background color in knitting worsted weight wool. 1 oz. or less of each of the following: dark brown, tan, yellow, dark green, red, blue, and light green.

NEEDLES: Size 4 and 7. One set of double-point needles size 4.

GAUGE: 5 sts = 1 inch, 6½ rows = 1 inch using knitting worsted.

SIZE: These directions are for a size 38″ finished garment. Measurements are as follows: length to underarm 15¾″, length to shoulder 25″, length of sleeve to underarm 18″.

To alter size see instructions for SIZING.

FRONT: With size 4 needles, cast on 80 sts. Work in K1, P1, ribbing for 3 inches. Change to size 7 needles and increase 8 sts evenly spaced on next row working in st st. Continue in st st and work the charted design, binding off and decreasing as indicated. Place the 14 sts in center of front on holder to be picked up later for neck ribbing.

BACK: Work back to match front deleting the sampler pattern but including the zig-zag pattern at the bottom. Place 24 sts in center of back on holder for neck ribbing.

SLEEVES: Cast on 40 sts on size 4 needles. Work in K1, P1, ribbing for 3 inches. Change to size 7 needles and increase 8 sts evenly spaced in next row using st st. Work sleeves according to charted design.

Sew shoulder seams.

NECK: With size 4 double-point needles, K across sts on back holder with right side facing. Pick up and K 56 sts to right shoulder (including sts on front holder). K1, P1, in ribbing on 80 sts for 1 inch. Bind off loosely in ribbing.

Sew sleeves in place. Sew underarm and sleeve seams. Weave in loose threads. Block lightly with damp cloth and warm iron.

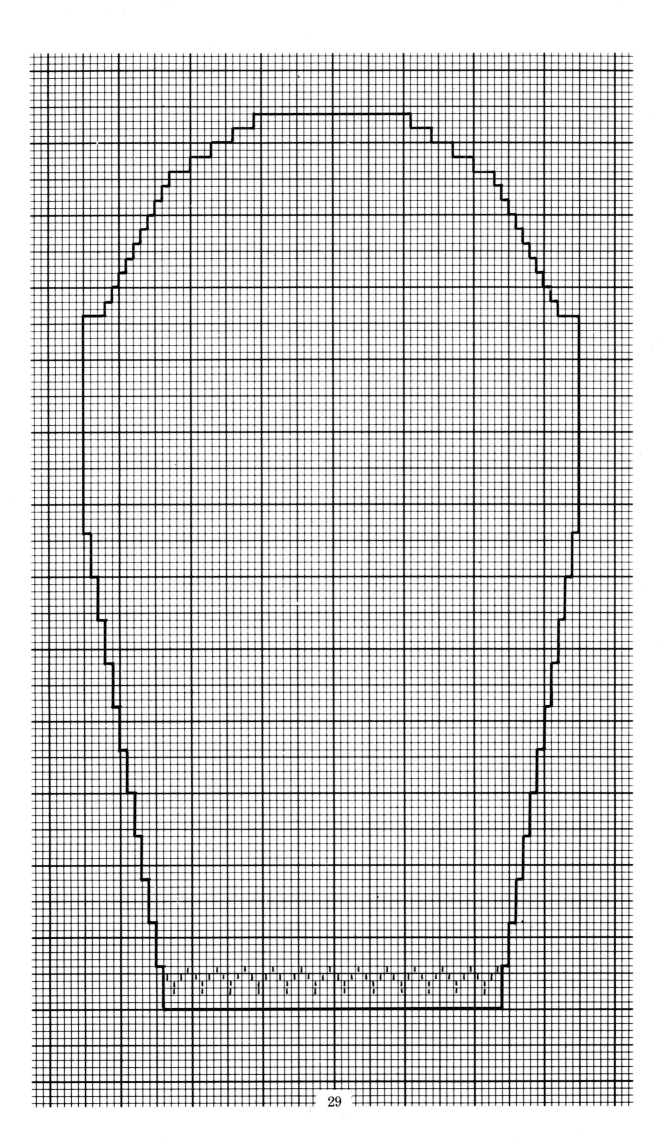

Tree-of-Life Crew-Neck Pullover

TREE-OF-LIFE CREW-NECK PULLOVER

A Tree-of-Life quilt pattern makes a wonderful band design on the front and back of this sweater with an overall diamond fleck. This motif is found in many variations on early 19th-century quilts.

MATERIALS: 20 to 22 oz. of main color in knitting worsted wool weight. 2 to 3 oz. of four contrasting colors, 4 oz. of another color for fleck and stripe.

NEEDLES: Size 4 and 7. One set of double-point needles size 4.

GAUGE: 5 sts = 1 inch, 6½ rows = 1 inch.

SIZE: These directions are for a size 38″ finished garment. Measurements are as follows: length to underarm 15¾″, length to shoulder 25″, length of sleeve to underarm 18″.

To alter size see instructions for SIZING.

FRONT: With size 4 needles, cast on 80 sts. Work in K1, P1, ribbing for 3 inches. Change to size 7 needles and increase 8 sts evenly spaced on next row working in st st. Continue in st st and work the charted design, binding off and decreasing as indicated. Place the 14 sts in center of front on holder to be picked up later for neck ribbing.

BACK: Work back to match front using charted pattern. Fill in pattern at neck with correlating designs and place 26 sts in center of back on holder for neck ribbing.

SLEEVES: Cast on 40 sts on size 4 needles. Work in K1, P1, ribbing for 3 inches. Change to size 7 needles and increase 8 sts evenly spaced in next row using st st. Work sleeves according to charted design.

Sew shoulder seams.

NECK: With size 4 double-point needles, K across sts on back holder with right side facing. Pick up and K 56 sts to right shoulder (including sts on front holder). K1, P1, in ribbing on 80 sts for 1 inch. Bind off loosely in ribbing.

Sew sleeves in place. Sew underarm and sleeve seams. Weave in loose threads. Block lightly with damp cloth and warm iron.

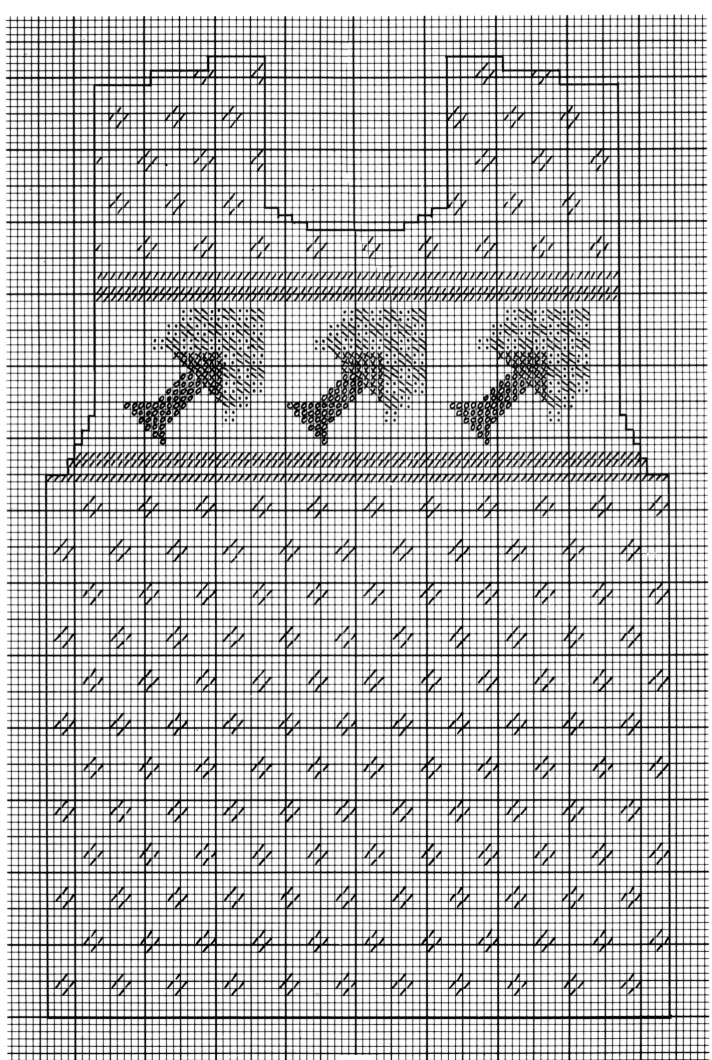

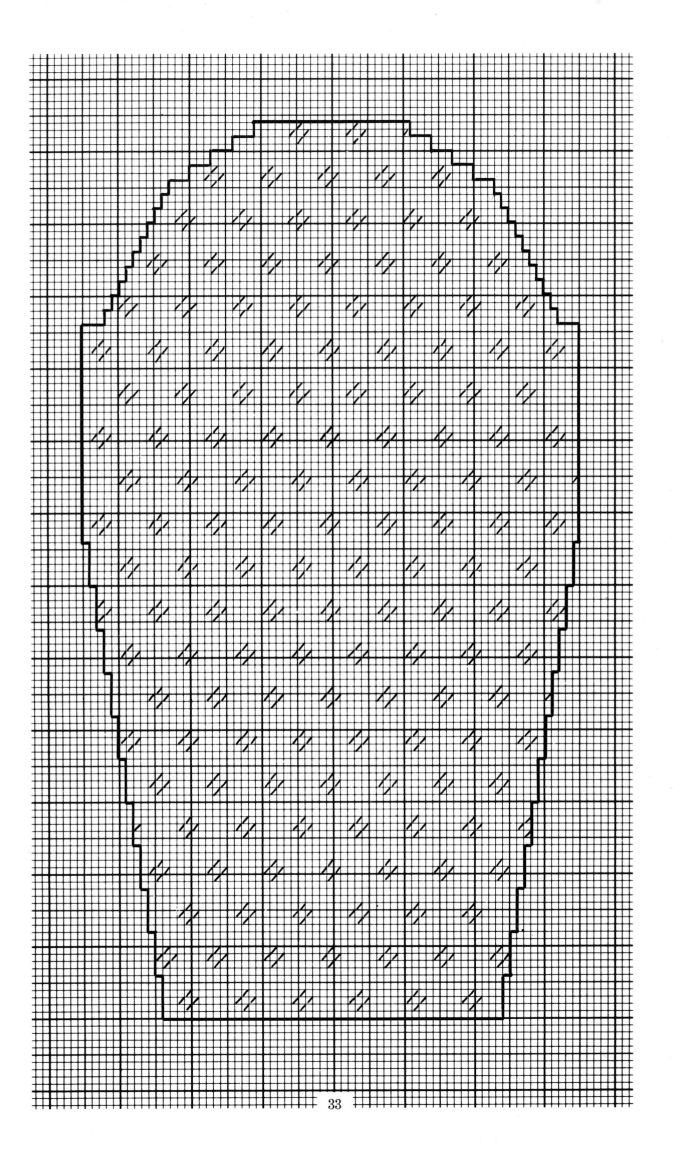

Basket Crew-Neck Pullover 1

BASKET CREW-NECK PULLOVER I

A patchwork-quilt pattern from the 19th century, this folk-art motif has retained its popularity and has been successfully used in many media. It is here adapted to a sweater with great appeal and charm.

MATERIALS: 16 to 18 oz. knitting worsted wool weight for background. 4 oz. color for diamonds. 6 oz. each of two colors for basket.

NEEDLES: Size 4 and 7. One set of double-point needles size 4.

GAUGE: 5 sts = 1 inch, 6½ rows = 1 inch.

SIZE: These directions are for a size 38" finished garment. Measurements are as follows: length to underarm 15¾", length to shoulder 25", length of sleeve to underarm 18".

To alter size see instructions for SIZING.

FRONT: With size 4 needles, cast on 80 sts. Work in K1, P1, ribbing for 3 inches. Change to size 7 needles and increase 8 sts evenly spaced on next row working in st st. Continue in st st and work the charted design, binding off and decreasing as indicated. Place the 14 sts in center of front on holder to be picked up later for neck ribbing.

BACK: Work back to match front. Fill in pattern at neck to shoulders and place 26 sts in center of back on holder for neck ribbing.

SLEEVES: Cast on 40 sts on size 4 needles. Work in K1, P1, ribbing for 3 inches. Change to size 7 needles and increase 8 sts evenly spaced in next row using st st. Work sleeves according to charted design.

Sew shoulder seams.

NECK: With size 4 double-point needles, K across sts on back holder with right side facing. Pick up and K 56 sts to right shoulder (including sts on front holder). K1, P1, in ribbing on 80 sts for 1 inch. Bind off loosely in ribbing.

Sew sleeves in place. Sew underarm and sleeve seams. Weave in loose threads. Block lightly with damp cloth and warm iron.

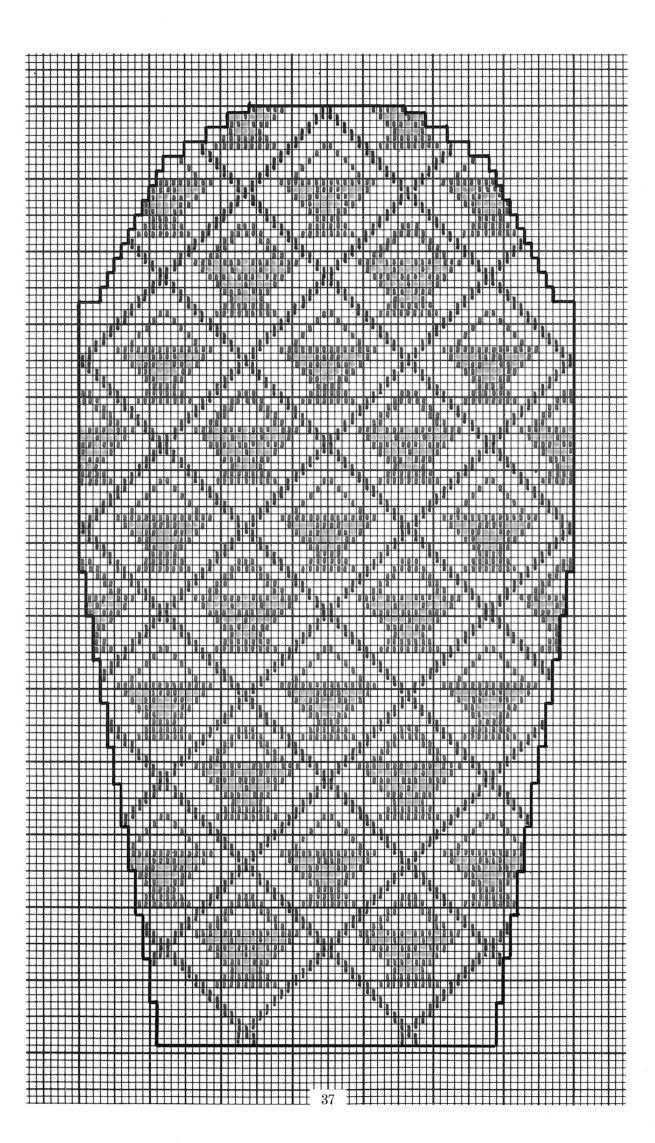

BASKET CREW-NECK PULLOVER II

The Basket pattern has proved so popular we have included a second pattern for use with lighter-weight yarns. It is super with cotton!

MATERIALS: 12 to 14 oz. main color in sport-weight wool or cotton. 4 oz. color for diamonds. 6 oz. each of two colors for basket.

NEEDLES: Size 2 and 5. One set of double-point needles size 2.

GAUGE: 5½ sts = 1 inch, 6½ rows = 1 inch.

SIZE: These directions are for a size 38″ finished garment. Measurements are as follows: length to underarm 16″, length to shoulder 24″, length of sleeve to underarm 17″.

To alter size see instructions for SIZING.

FRONT: With size 2 needles, cast on 96 sts. Work in K2, P2, ribbing for 3 inches. Change to size 5 needles and increase 12 sts evenly spaced on next row working in st st. Continue in st st and work the charted design, binding off and decreasing as indicated. Place the 28 sts in center of front on holder to be picked up later for neck ribbing.

BACK: Work back to match front. Fill in pattern at neck to shoulders and place 26 sts in center of back on holder for neck ribbing.

SLEEVES: With size 2 needles, cast on 42 sts. Work in K2, P2, ribbing for 3 inches. Change to size 5 needles and increase 8 sts evenly spaced in next row using st st. Work sleeves according to charted design.

Sew shoulder seams.

NECK: With size 2 double-point needles and right side facing, pick up and K across 34 sts on back holder, pick up and K 13 sts to front holder, K across 28 sts on front holder, and pick up and K 13 sts to back. Total of 88 sts. K2, P2, in ribbing for 1 inch.

Sew sleeves in place. Sew underarm and sleeve seams. Weave in loose threads. Block lightly with damp cloth and warm iron.

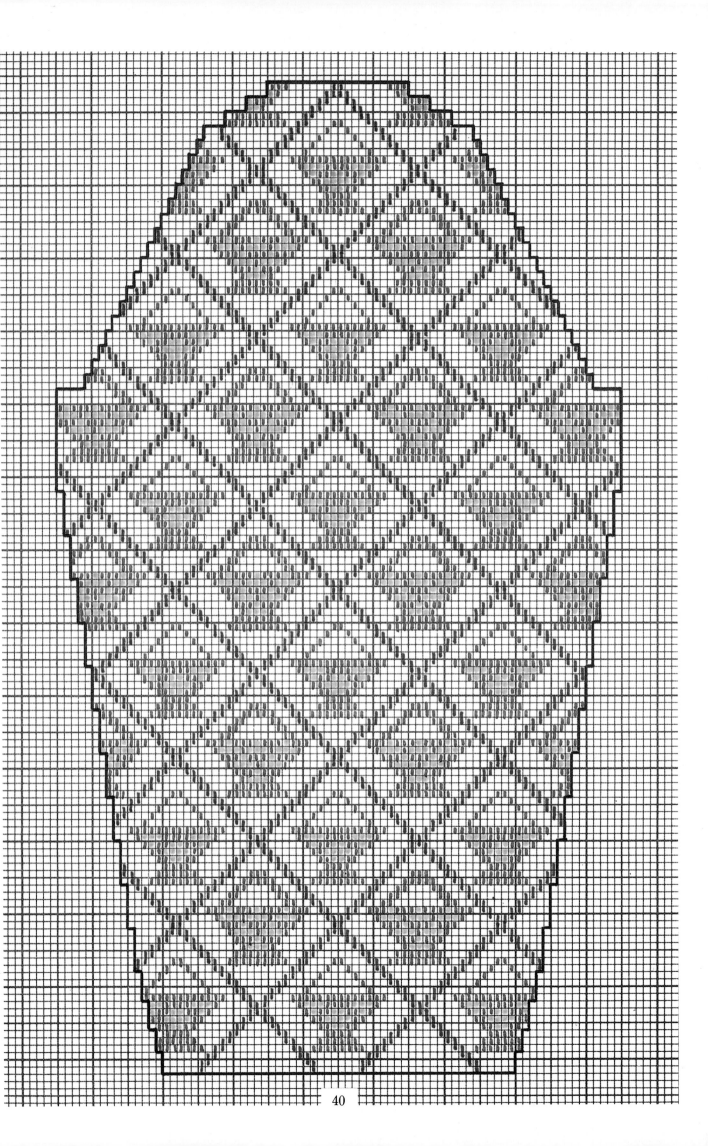

Plaid Blanket Sleeveless Vest

PLAID BLANKET SLEEVELESS VEST

Taken from an 18th-century blue-and-white woven blanket, this pattern works up beautifully into a traditional vest. Quick and fun to make, it will become a wardrobe classic.

MATERIALS: 5 to 6 oz. each of two contrasting colors in sport-weight wool or cotton.

NEEDLES: Size 2 and 5. One set of double-point needles, size 2.

GAUGE: 6 sts = 1 inch, 7 rows = 1 inch.

SIZE: These directions are for a size 36″ finished garment. Measurements are: length to underarm 14″, length to shoulder 21½″.

To alter size see instructions for SIZING.

FRONT: With size 2 needles, cast on 83 sts. Work in K1, P1, ribbing for 3 inches. Change to size 5 needles and increase 10 sts evenly spaced on next row working in st st. Continue in st st and work the charted design, binding off and decreasing as indicated. Place the center st on a holder to be picked up later.

BACK: Work to match front, omitting V-neck and filling in pattern to shoulders. Place 35 center sts of back on holder for neck ribbing.

Sew shoulder seams.

NECK: With size 2 double-point needles, pick up and K 35 sts from back holder, 54 sts from right front, center st of V (mark), and 54 sts from left front (right side facing). Work as follows:
Row 1: K1, P1, repeat to within 2 sts of marked st. K2 tog, P1, K2 tog, begin with P1 in ribbing across.
Row 2: Work in ribbing, dec 1 st each side of marked st.
Repeat these 2 rows 3 times.
Bind off loosely in ribbing.

ARMHOLES: With size 2 needles, pick up and K 100 sts with right side facing. Work in K1, P1, ribbing for 5 rows. Bind off loosely in ribbing.

Sew armhole and side seams. Weave in loose threads. Block lightly with damp cloth and warm iron.

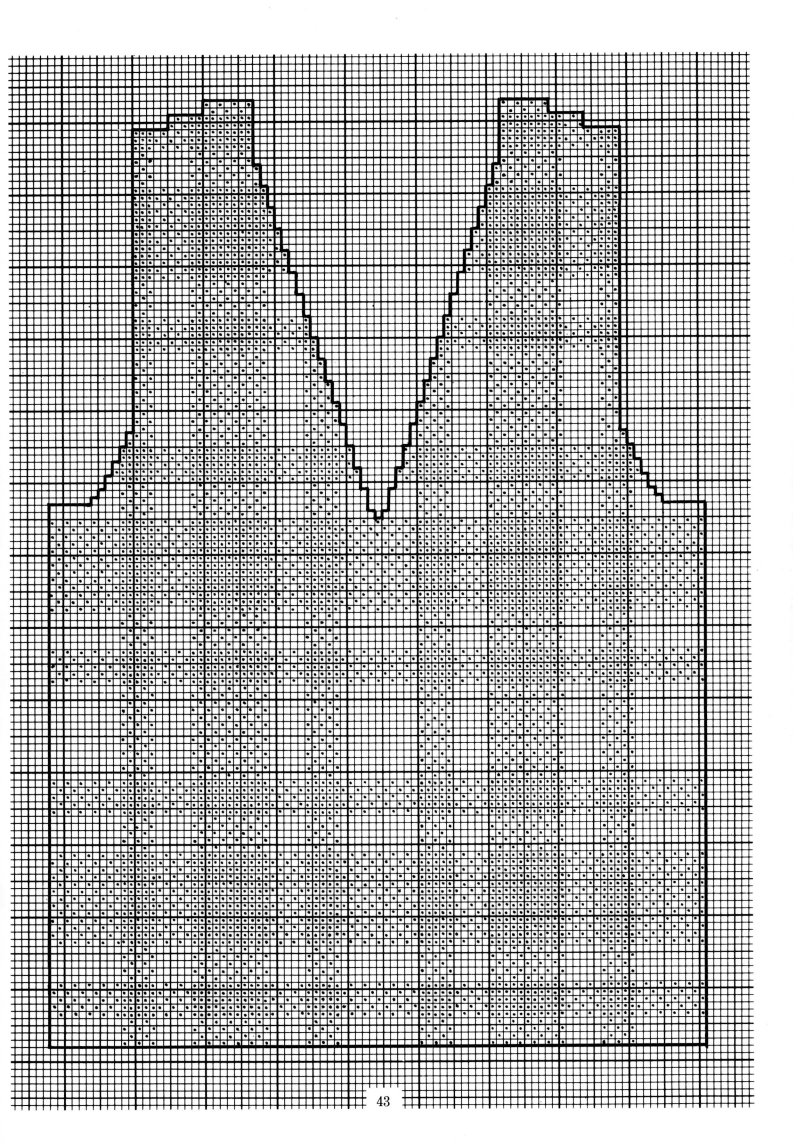

Shaker Tree-of-Life Crew-Neck Pullover

SHAKER TREE-OF-LIFE CREW-NECK PULLOVER

This famous Shaker artwork was painted by Sister Hannah Cohoon in 1854. It has been transcribed for this sweater as a central motif that can be placed on the front or back. A popular and pleasing design.

MATERIALS: 20 to 22 oz. of main color in knitting worsted wool weight. 2 oz. of a contrasting color.

NEEDLES: Size 4 and 7. One set of double-point needles, size 4.

GAUGE: 5 sts = 1 inch, 6½ rows = 1 inch.

SIZE: These directions are for a size 38″ finished garment. Measurements are as follows: length to underarm 15¾″, length to shoulder 25″, length of sleeve to underarm 18″.

To alter size see instructions for SIZING.

FRONT: With size 4 needles, cast on 80 sts. Work in K1, P1, ribbing for 3 inches. Change to size 7 needles and increase 8 sts evenly spaced on next row working in st st. Continue in st st and work the charted design, binding off and decreasing as indicated. Place the 14 sts in center of front on holder to be picked up later for ribbing.

BACK: Work back to match front omitting design. Fill in pattern at neck to shoulders and place 26 sts in center of back on holder for neck ribbing.

SLEEVES: Cast on 40 sts on size 4 needles. Work in K1, P1, ribbing for 3 inches. Change to size 7 needles and increase 8 sts evenly spaced in next row using st st. Work sleeves according to outline of sleeve for Sampler Crew Neck Pullover, omitting the zig-zag design.

Sew shoulder seams.

NECK: With size 4 double-point needles, K across sts on back holder with right side facing. Pick up and K 56 sts to right shoulder (including sts on front holder). K1, P1, in ribbing on 80 sts for 1 inch. Bind off loosely in ribbing.

Sew sleeves in place. Sew underarm and sleeve seams. Weave in loose threads. Block lightly with damp cloth and warm iron.

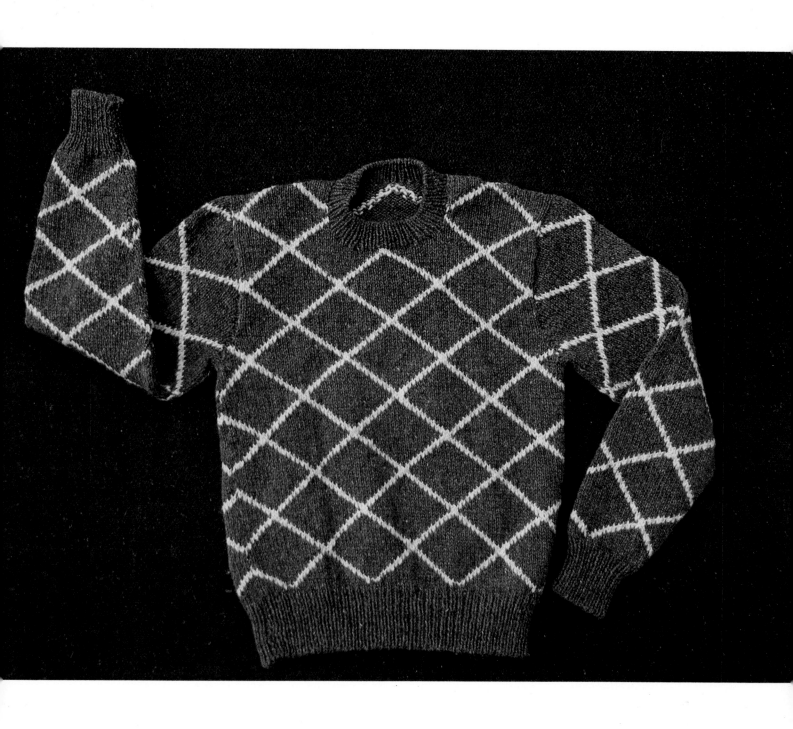

Diamonds Crew-Neck Pullover

DIAMONDS CREW-NECK PULLOVER

Based on early woven blanket, this pattern is a classic. It looks great in any color, and is easy to knit.

MATERIALS: 20 to 22 oz. main color in knitting worsted wool. 4 oz. of a contrasting color.

NEEDLES: Size 4 and 7. One set of double-point needles, size 4.

GAUGE: 5 sts = 1 inch, 6½ rows = 1 inch.

SIZE: These directions are for a size 38" finished garment. Measurements are as follows: length to underarm 15¾", length to shoulder 25", length of sleeve to underarm 18".

To alter size see instructions for SIZING.

FRONT: With size 4 needles, cast on 80 sts. Work in K1, P1, ribbing for 3 inches. Change to size 7 needles and increase 8 sts evenly spaced on next row working in st st. Continue in st st and work the charted design, binding off and decreasing as indicated. Place the 14 sts in center of front on holder to be picked up later for neck ribbing.

BACK: Work back to match front. Fill in pattern at neck to shoulders and place 26 sts in center of back on holder for neck ribbing.

SLEEVES: Cast on 40 sts on size 4 needles. Work in K1, P1, ribbing for 3 inches. Change to size 7 needles and increase 8 sts evenly spaced in next row using st st. Work sleeves according to charted design.

Sew shoulder seams.

NECK: With size 4 double-point needles, K across sts on back holder with right side facing. Pick up K 56 sts to right shoulder (including sts on front holder). K1, P1, in ribbiing on 80 sts for 1 inch. Bind off loosely in ribbing.

Sew sleeves in place. Sew underarm and sleeve seams. Weave in loose threads. Block lightly with damp cloth and warm iron.

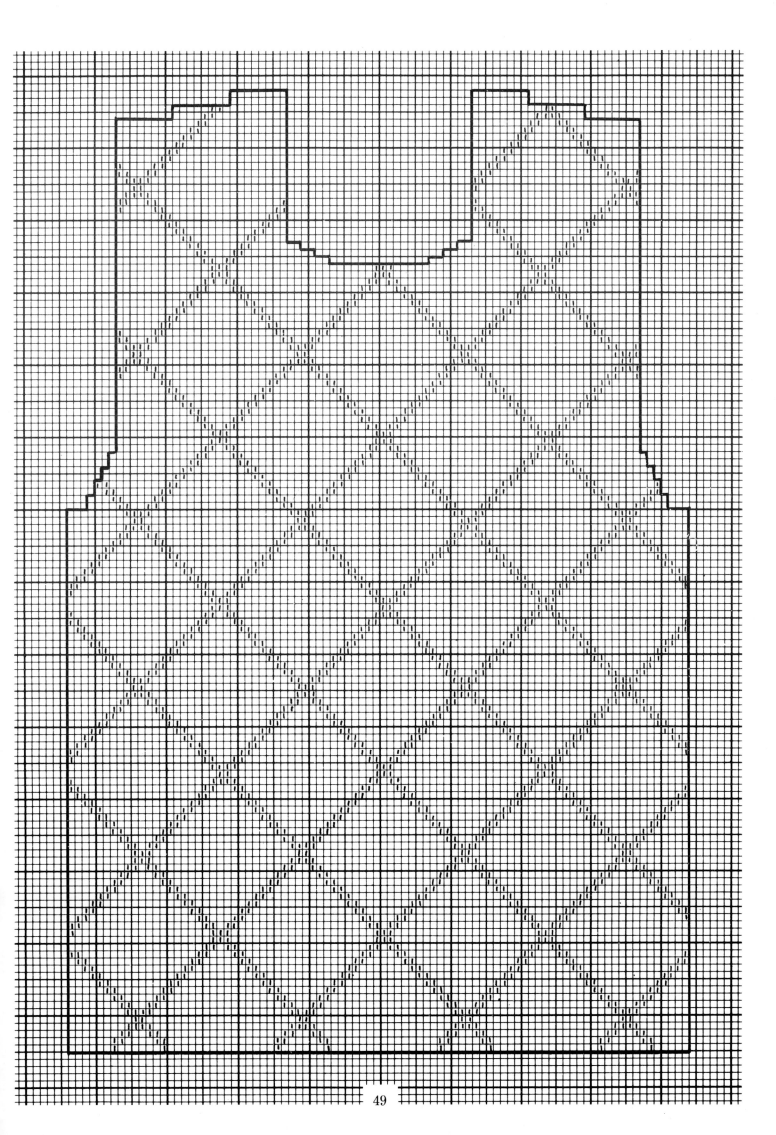

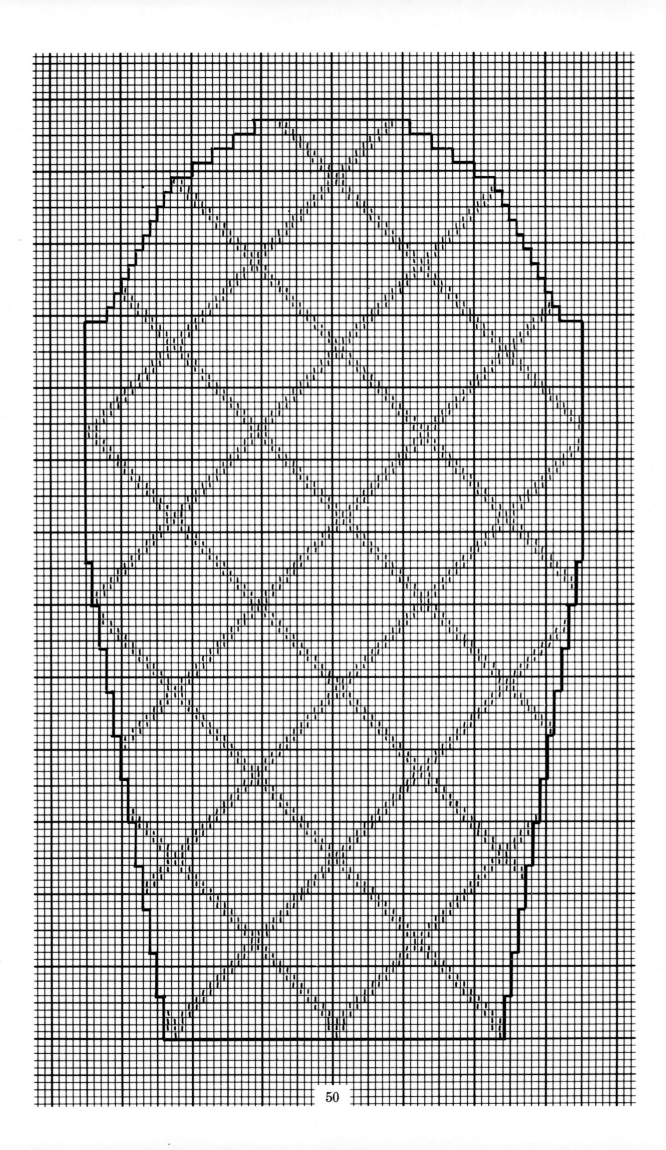

Patchwork Sampler
Crew-Neck Pullover

PATCHWORK SAMPLER CREW-NECK PULLOVER

A patchwork array of folk-art motifs separated by bands of solid color make this sweater a delightful sampler. Inspired by similar quilt patterns and sampler designs, this is a great method to use up yarn leftovers and achieve a super country look.

MATERIALS: 14 to 16 oz. background color in knitting worsted wool. 4 to 6 oz. color for solid bands. Various amounts of several colors for designs inside blocks.

NEEDLES: Size 4 and 7. One set of double point needles, size 4.

GAUGE: 5 sts = 1 inch, 6½ rows = 1 inch.

SIZE: These directions are for a size 38″ finished garment. Measurements are as follows: length to underarm 15¾″, length to shoulder 25″, length of sleeve to underarm 18″.

To alter size see instructions for SIZING.

FRONT: With size 4 needles, cast on 80 sts. Work in K1, P1, ribbing for 3 inches. Change to size 7 needles and increase 8 sts evenly spaced on next row working in st st. Continue in st st and work the charted design, binding off and decreasing as indicated. Place the 14 sts in center of front on holder to be picked up later for neck ribbing.

BACK: Work back to match front. Fill in pattern at neck to shoulders and place 26 sts in center of back on holder for neck ribbing.

SLEEVES: Cast on 40 sts on size 4 needles. Work in K1, P1, ribbing for 3 inches. Change to size 7 needles and increase 8 sts evenly spaced in next row using st st. Work sleeves according to charted design.

Sew shoulder seams.

NECK: With size 4 double-point needles, K across sts on back holder with right side facing. Pick up and K 56 sts to right shoulder (including sts on front holder). K1, P1, in ribbing on 80 sts for 1 inch. Bind off loosely in ribbing.

Sew sleeves in place. Sew underarm and sleeve seams. Weave in loose threads. Block lightly with damp cloth and warm iron.

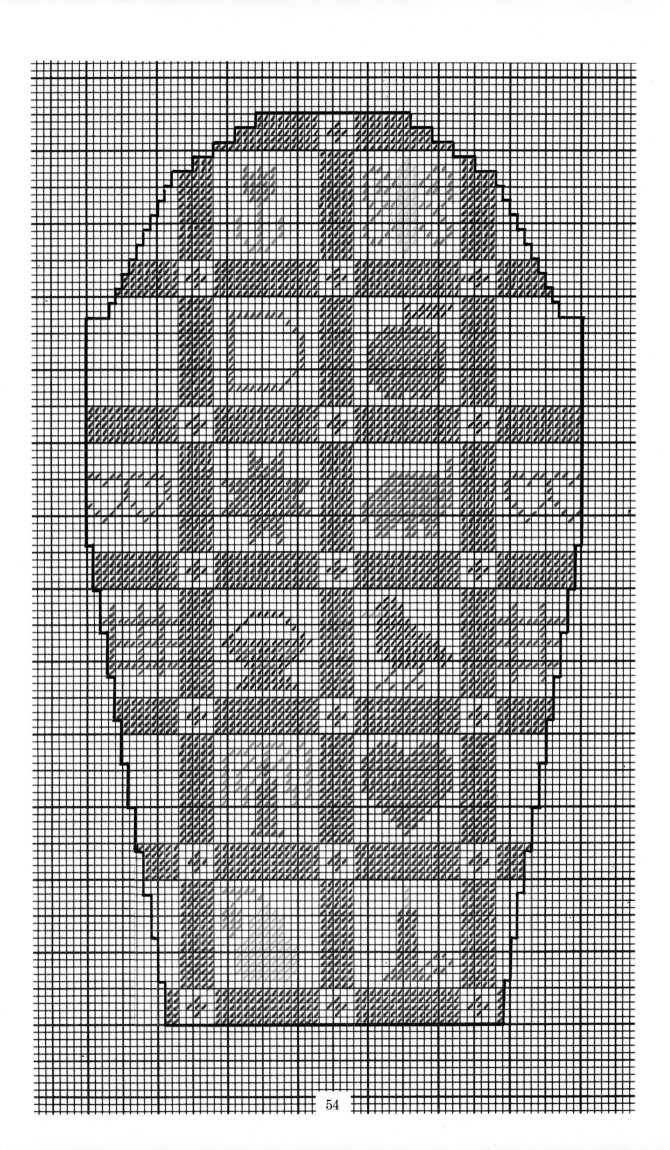

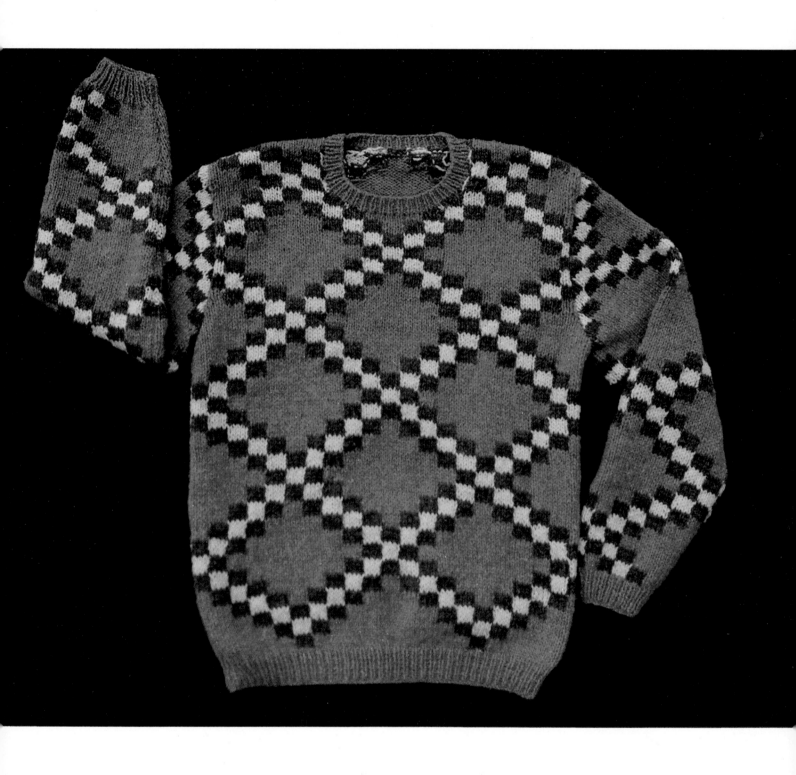

Double Irish Chain
Crew-Neck Pullover

DOUBLE IRISH CHAIN CREW-NECK PULLOVER

A familiar quilt design, this bold pattern works up into a dynamite sweater. Originally dating from the mid-19th century, this pattern makes a wonderful alternative to a classic argyle.

MATERIALS: 18 to 20 oz. of knitting worsted wool weight main color. 6 to 8 oz. of contrasting color for center squares. 12 to 14 oz. of a contrasting color for outside squares.

NEEDLES: Size 4 and 7. One set of double-point needles, size 4.

GAUGE: 5 sts = 1 inch, 6½ rows = 1 inch.

SIZE: These directions are for a size 38″ finished garment. Measurements are as follows: length to underarm 15¾″, length to shoulder 25″, length of sleeve to underarm 18″.

To alter size see instructions for SIZING.

FRONT: With size 4 needles, cast on 80 sts. Work in K1, P1, ribbing for 3 inches. Change to size 7 needles and increase 8 sts evenly spaced on next row working in st st. Continue in st st and work the charted design, binding off and decreasing as indicated. Place the 14 sts in center of front on holder to be picked up later for neck ribbing.

BACK: Work back to match front. Fill in pattern at neck to shoulders and place 26 sts in center of back on holder for neck ribbing.

SLEEVES: Cast on 40 sts on size 4 needles. Work in K1, P1, ribbing for 3 inches. Change to size 7 needles and increase 8 sts evenly spaced in next row using st st. Work sleeves according to charted design.

Sew shoulder seams.

NECK: With size 4 double-point needles, K across sts on back holder with right side facing. Pick up and K 56 sts to right shoulder (including sts on front holder). K1, P1, in ribbing on 80 sts for 1 inch. Bind off loosely in ribbing.

Sew sleeves in place. Sew underarm and sleeve seams. Weave in loose threads. Block lightly with damp cloth and warm iron.

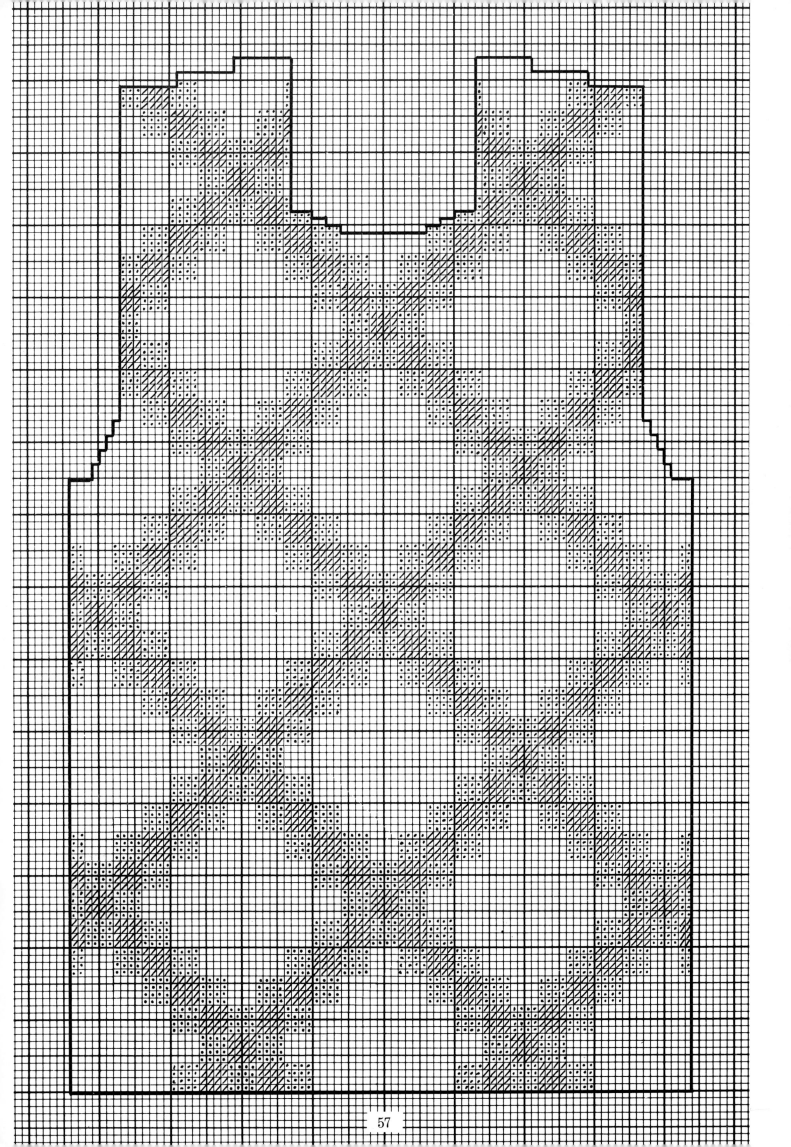

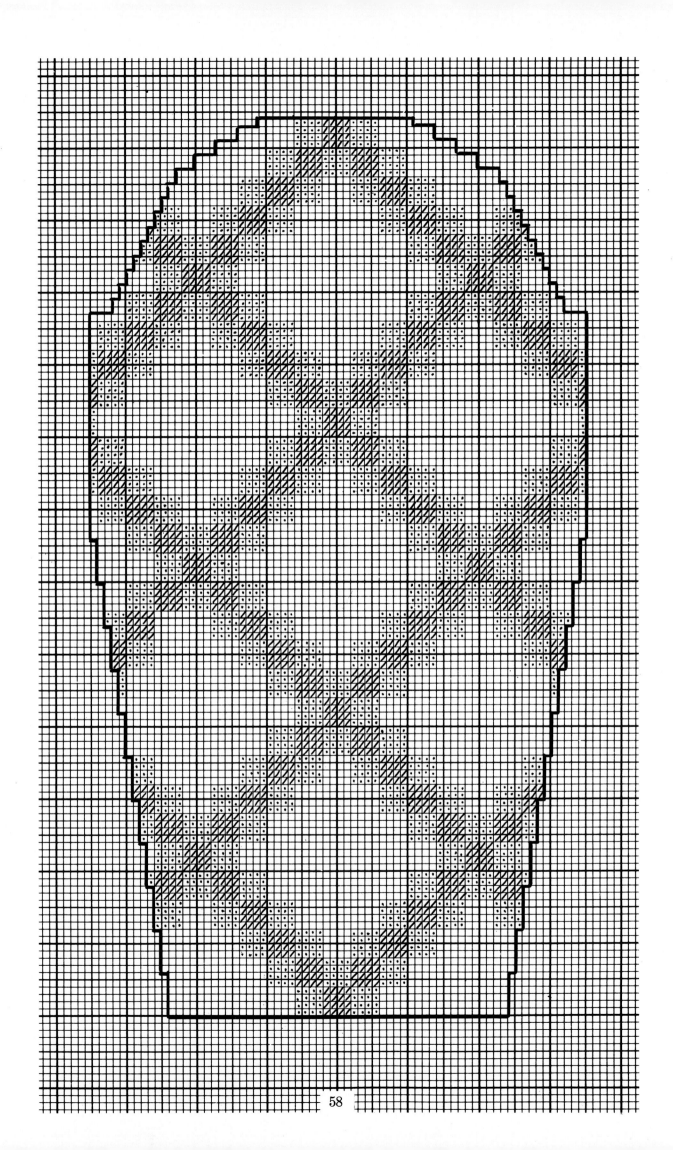

SAMPLER SLEEVELESS VEST

A center-hall Colonial house is the star attraction of this simple and quick-to-knit little vest. A popular pattern adapted from samplers and other folk-art needlework.

MATERIALS: 8 to 9 oz. of main color in sport-weight wool or cotton. 1 to 2 oz. of 4 contrasting colors for house, windows, trees, and fence.

NEEDLES: Size 2 and 5. One set of double-point needles, size 2.

GAUGE: 6 sts = 1 inch, 7 rows = 1 inch.

SIZE: These directions are for a size 36″ finished garment. Measurements are as follows: length to underarm 14″, length to shoulder 21½″.

To alter size see instructions for SIZING.

FRONT: With size 2 needles, cast on 83 sts. Work in K1, P1, ribbing for 3 inches. Change to size 5 needles and increase 10 sts evenly spaced on next row working in st st. Continue in st st and work the charted design, binding off and decreasing as indicated. Place the center st on a holder to be picked up later.

BACK: Work to match front, omitting V-neck and filling in pattern to shoulders. Place 35 center sts of back on holder for neck ribbing.

Sew shoulder seams.

NECK: With size 2 double-point needles, pick up and K 35 sts from back holder, 54 sts from right front, center st of V (mark), and 54 sts from left front (right side facing). Work as follows:
Row 1: K1, P1, repeat to within 2 sts of marked st. K2 tog, P1, K2 tog, begin with P1 in ribbing across.
Row 2: Work in ribbing, dec 1 st each side of marked st.
Repeat these 2 rows 3 times.
Bind off loosely in ribbing.

ARMHOLES: With size 2 needles, pick up and K 100 sts with right side facing. Work in K1, P1, ribbing for 5 rows. Bind off loosely in ribbing.

Sew armholes and side seams. Weave in loose threads. Block lightly with damp cloth and warm iron.

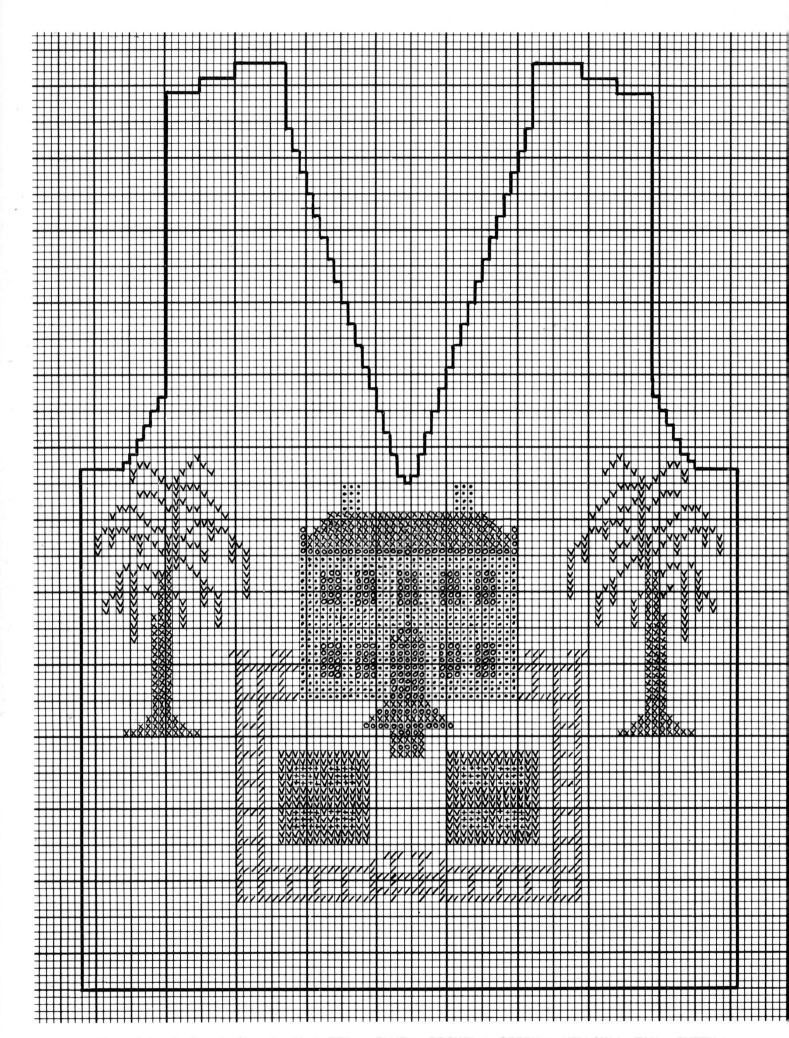

Key to Colors for Sampler Sleeveless Vest   RED •   BLUE ◦   BROWN ✗   GREEN ⋁   YELLOW ✚   TAN or PUTTY ⁄

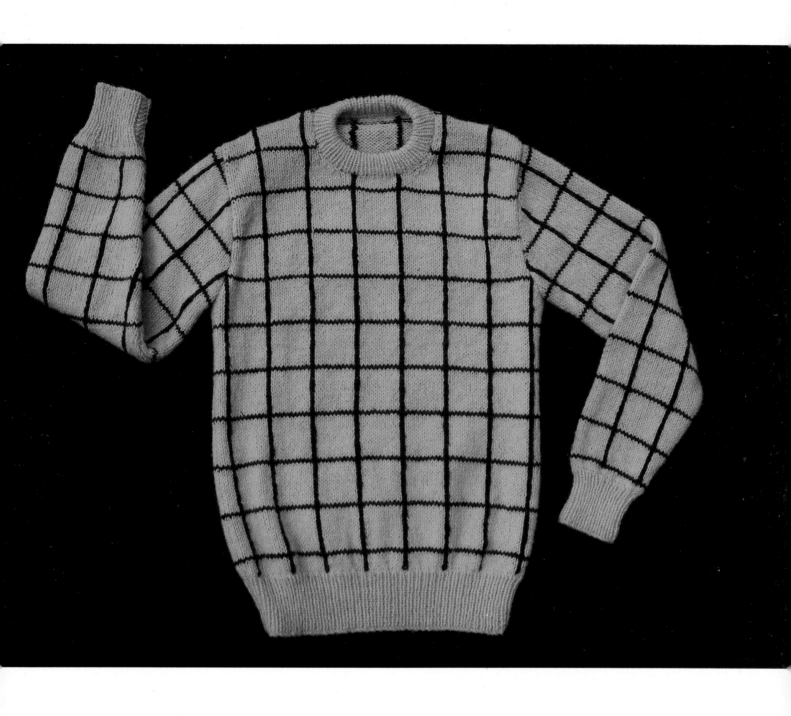

Windowpane Crew-Neck Pullover

WINDOWPANE CREW-NECK PULLOVER

A typical design used by the Shakers for woven twill blankets. The background was always white and the horizontal and vertical lines usually blue (dyed with indigo) and/or red (dyed with madder). A classic design for a classic sweater.

MATERIALS: 20 to 22 oz. main color in knitting worsted wool. 3 to 4 oz. of a contrasting color.

NEEDLES: Size 4 and 7. One set of double-point needles, size 4.

GAUGE: 5 sts = 1 inch, 6½ rows = 1 inch.

SIZE: These directions are for a size 38″ finished garment. Measurements are as follows: length to underarm 15¾″, length to shoulder 25″, length of sleeve to underarm 18″.

To alter size see instructions for SIZING.

FRONT: With size 4 needles, cast on 80 sts. Work in K1, P1, ribbing for 3 inches. Change to size 7 needles and increase 8 sts evenly spaced on next row working in st st. Continue in st st and work the charted design, binding off and decreasing as indicated. Place the 14 sts in center of front on holder to be picked up later for neck ribbing.

BACK: Work back to match front. Fill in pattern at neck to shoulders and place 26 sts in center of back on holder for neck ribbing.

SLEEVES: Cast on 40 sts on size 4 needles. Work in K1, P1, ribbing for 3 inches. Change to size 7 needles and increase 8 sts evenly spaced in next row using st st. Work sleeves according to charted design.

Sew shoulder seams.

NECK: With size 4 double-point needles, K across sts on back holder with right side facing. Pick up and K 56 sts to right shoulder (including sts on front holder). K1, P1, in ribbing on 80 sts for 1 inch. Bind off loosely in ribbing.

Sew sleeves in place. Sew underarm and sleeve seams. Weave in loose threads. Block lightly with damp cloth and warm iron.

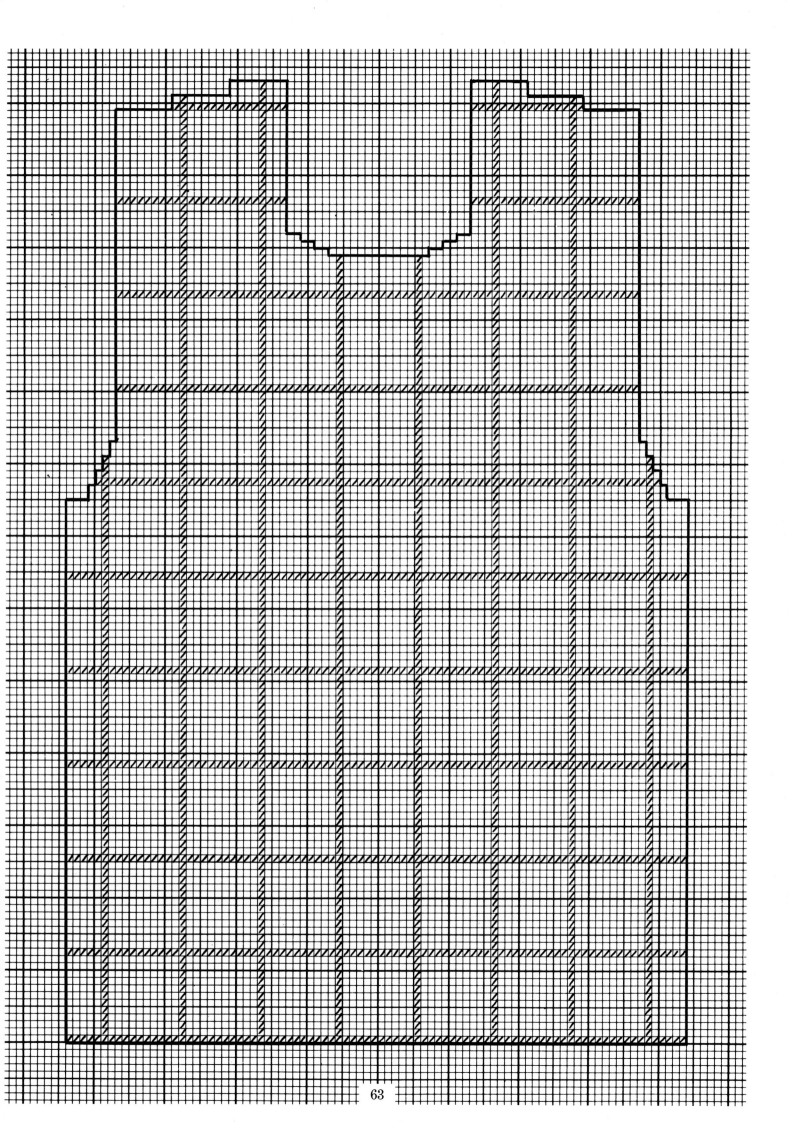

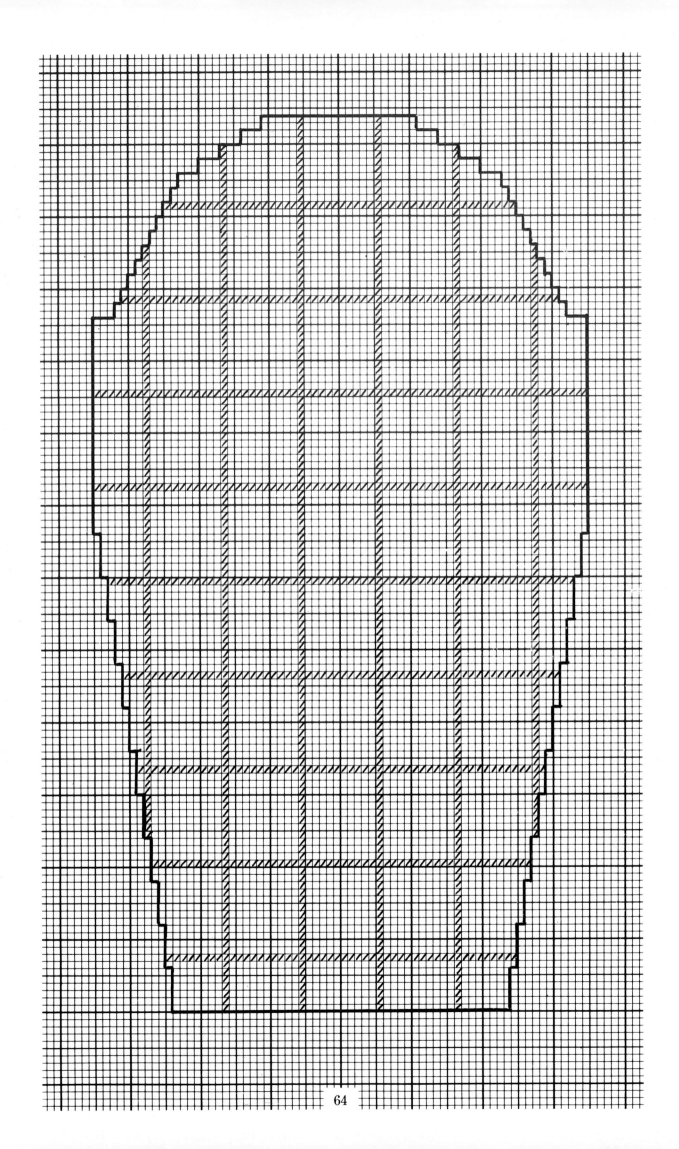

Log Cabin Crew-Neck Pullover

LOG CABIN CREW-NECK PULLOVER

There are hundreds of variations of the Log Cabin quilt pattern. Created in the last half of the 19th century, it incorporates many odd bits of fabric into a very graphic arrangement of lights and darks. Adapted to a sweater, the pattern is visually striking, and a great way to use up odd bits of yarn.

MATERIALS: 4 to 6 oz. of 6 different colors of knitting worsted wool.

NEEDLES: Size 4 and 7. One set of double-pointed needles, size 4.

GAUGE: 5 sts = 1 inch, 6½ rows = 1 inch.

SIZE: These directions are for a size 38″ finished garment. Measurements are as follows: length to underarm 15¾″, length to shoulder 25″, length of sleeve to underarm 18″.

To alter size see instructions for SIZING.

FRONT: With size 4 needles, cast on 80 sts. Work K1, P1, ribbing for 3 inches. Change to size 7 needles and increase 8 sts evenly spaced on next row working in st st. Continue in st st and work the charted design, binding off and decreasing as indicated. Place the 14 sts in center of front on holder to be picked up later for neck ribbing.

BACK: Work back to match front. Fill in pattern at neck to shoulders and place 26 sts in center of back on holder for neck ribbing.

SLEEVES: Cast on 40 sts on size 4 needles. Work in K1, P1, ribbing for 3 inches. Change to size 7 needles and increase 8 sts evenly spaced in next row using st st. Work sleeves according to charted design.

Sew shoulder seams.

NECK: With size 4 double-point needles, K across sts on back holder with right side facing. Pick up and K 56 sts to right shoulder (including sts on front holder). K1, P1, in ribbing on 80 sts for 1 inch. Bind off loosely in ribbing.

Sew sleeves in place. Sew underarm and sleeve seams. Weave in loose threads. Block lightly with damp cloth and warm iron.

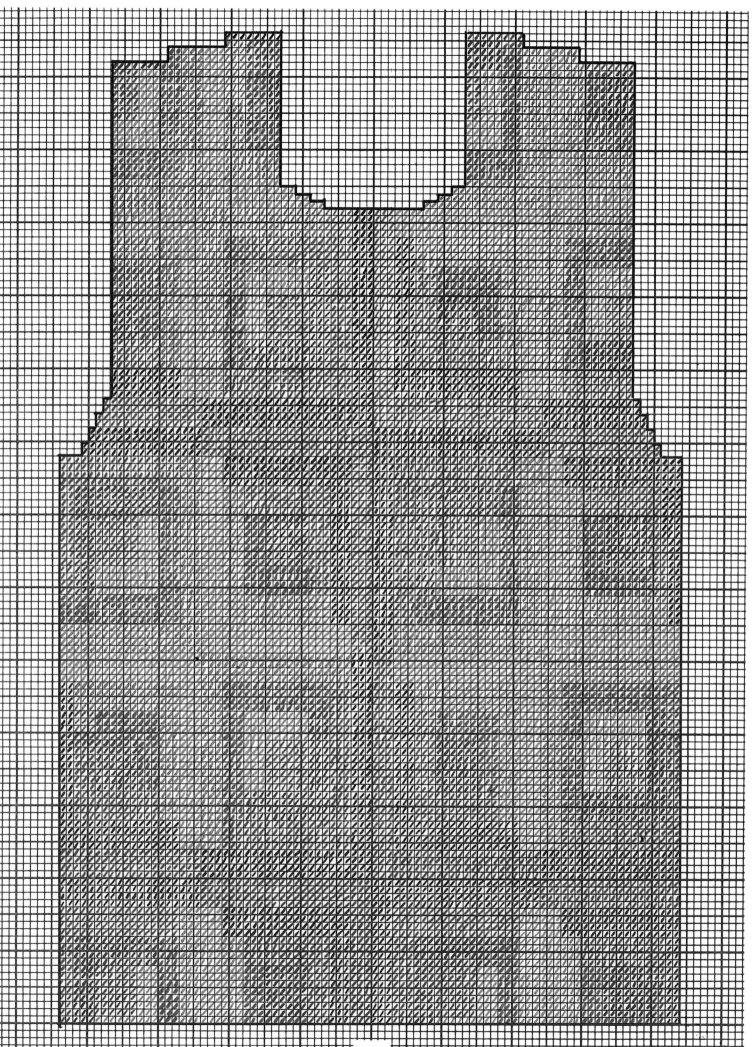

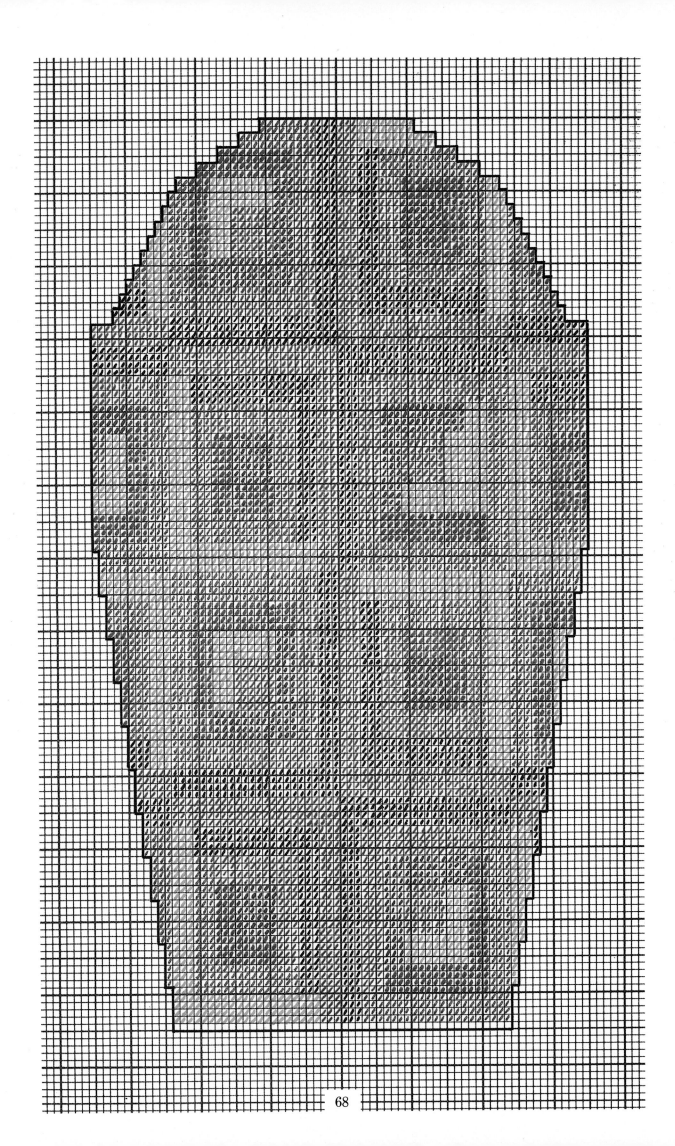

Shaker Blanket Crew-Neck Pullover

SHAKER BLANKET CREW-NECK PULLOVER

The Shakers were famous for their woven textiles. This is an adaptation of one of their beautiful blankets. An interesting pattern and easy to knit, it makes into a striking garment.

MATERIALS: 10 to 12 oz. white in sport-weight wool or cotton. 6 to 8 oz. each of two contrasting colors.

NEEDLES: Size 2 and 5. One set of double-pointed needles, size 2.

GAUGE: 5½ sts = 1 inch, 6½ rows = 1 inch.

SIZE: These directions are for a size 38″ finished garment. Measurements are as follows: length to underarm 16″, length to shoulder 24″, length of sleeve to underarm 17″.

To alter size see instructions for SIZING.

FRONT: With size 2 needles, cast on 96 sts. Work in K2, P2, ribbing for 3 inches. Change to size 5 needles and increase 12 sts evenly spaced on next row working in st st. Continue in st st and work the charted design, binding off and decreasing as indicated. Place the 28 sts in center of front on holder to be picked up later for neck ribbing.

BACK: Work back to match front. Fill in pattern at neck to shoulders and place 34 sts in center of back on holder for neck ribbing.

SLEEVES: With size 2 needles, cast on 42 sts. Work in K2, P2, ribbing for 3 inches. Change to size 5 needles and increase 8 sts evenly spaced in next row using st st. Work sleeves according to charted design.

Sew shoulder seams.

NECK: With size 2 double-point needles and right side facing, pick up and K across sts on back holder (34), pick up and K 13 sts to front holder, K across 28 sts on front holder, and pick up and K 13 sts to back. Total of 88 sts. K2, P2, in ribbing for 1 inch.

Sew sleeves in place. Sew underarm and sleeve seams. Weave in loose threads. Block lightly with damp cloth and warm iron.

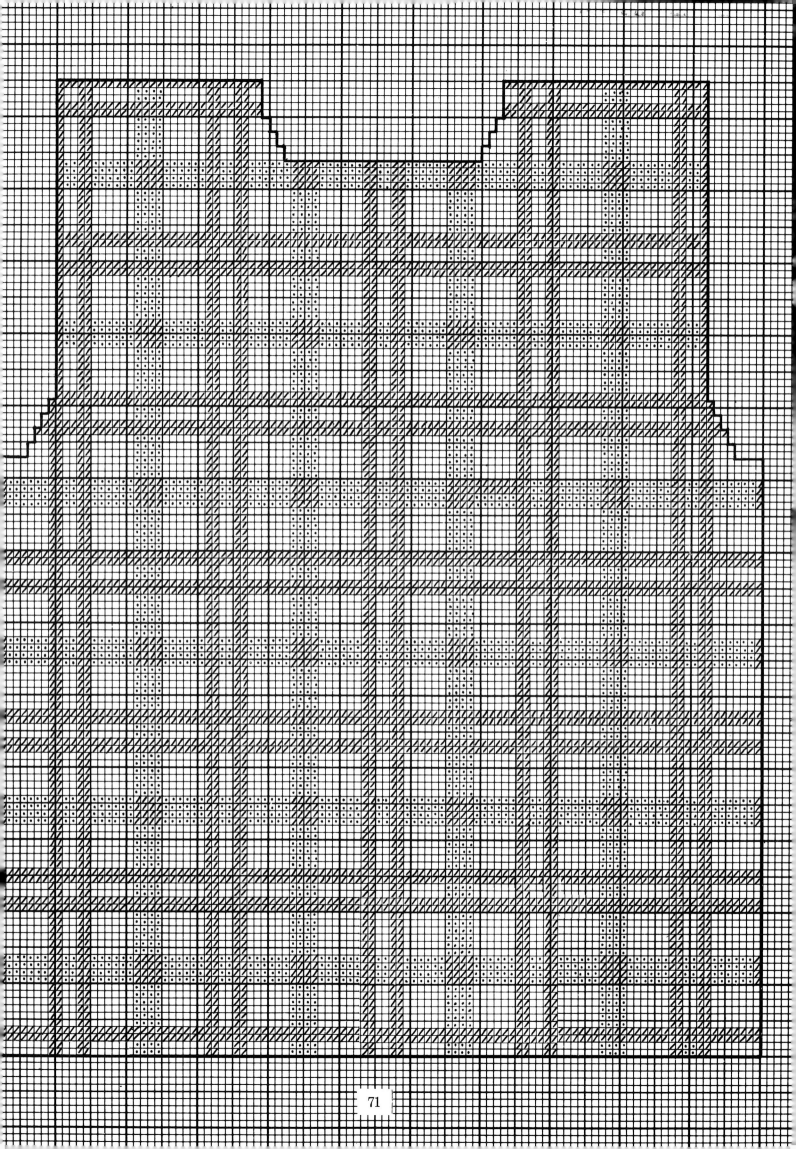

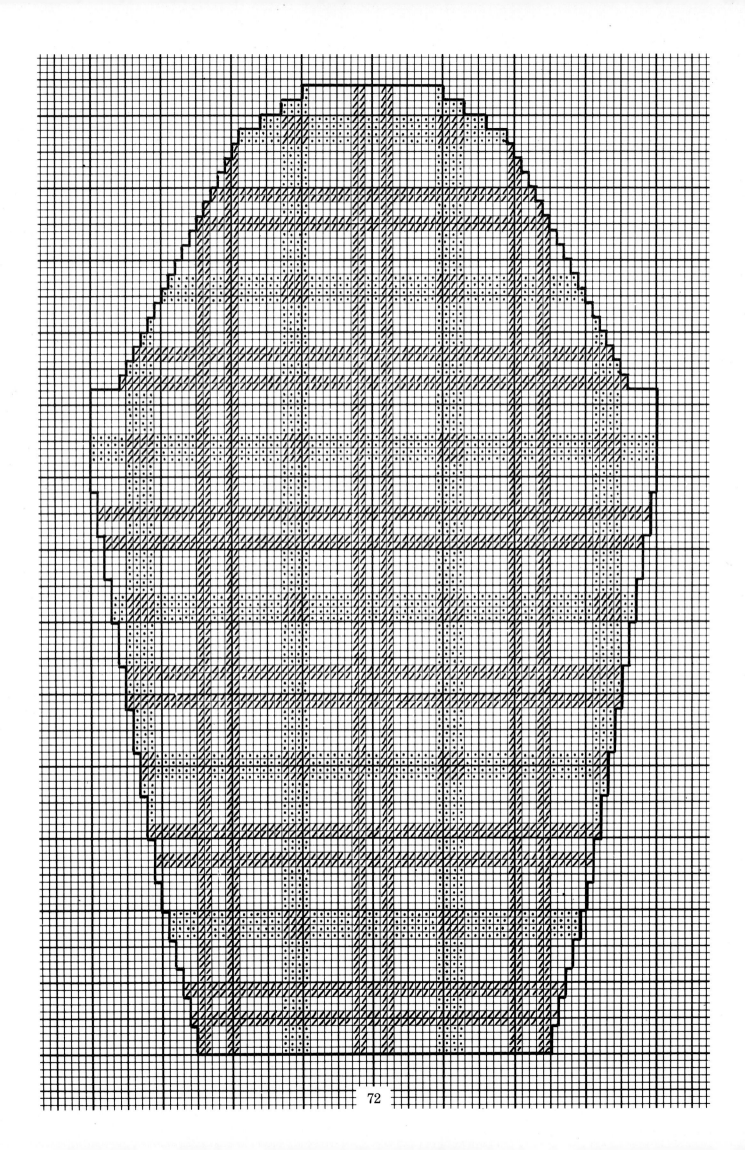

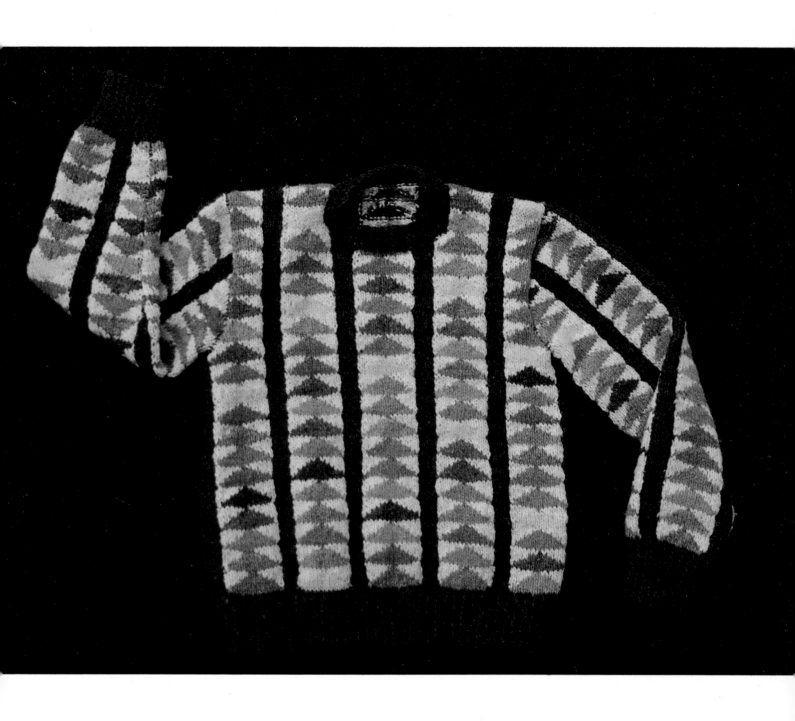

Flying Geese Crew-Neck Pullover

FLYING GEESE CREW-NECK PULLOVER

A colorful and exciting pattern based on a popular 19th-century quilt pattern called Flying Geese. This design was often made with oddments of fabric left from various sewing projects. It was also worked as a three-color quilt: the background is one color, bands another, and triangles a third. Whichever color scheme you choose, this will be one of your favorites.

MATERIALS: 8 oz. knitting worsted wool-weight for stripes. 8 oz. for background color. 8 oz. of various colors or same color for triangles.

NEEDLES: Size 4 and 7. One set of double-point needles, size 4.

GAUGE: 5 sts = 1 inch, 6½ rows = 1 inch.

SIZE: These directions are for a size 38″ finished garment. Measurements are as follows: length to underarm 15¾″, length to shoulder 25″, length of sleeve to underarm 18″.

To alter size see instructions for SIZING.

FRONT: With size 4 needles, cast on 80 sts. Work in K1, P1, ribbing for 3 inches. Change to size 7 needles and increase 8 sts evenly spaced on next row working in st st. Continue in st st and work the charted design, binding off and decreasing as indicated. Place the 14 sts in center of front on holder to be picked up later for neck ribbing.

BACK: Work back to match front. Fill in pattern at neck to shoulders and place 26 sts in center of back on holder for neck ribbing.

SLEEVES: Cast on 40 sts on size 4 needles. Work in K1, P1, ribbing for 3 inches. Change to size 7 needles and increase 8 sts evenly spaced in next row using st st. Work sleeves according to charted design.

Sew shoulder seams.

NECK: With size 4 double-point needles, K across sts on back holder with right side facing. Pick up and K 56 sts to right shoulder (including sts on front holder). K1, P1, in ribbing on 80 sts for 1 inch. Bind off loosely in ribbing.

Sew sleeves in place. Sew underarm and sleeve seams. Weave in loose threads. Block lightly with damp cloth and warm iron.

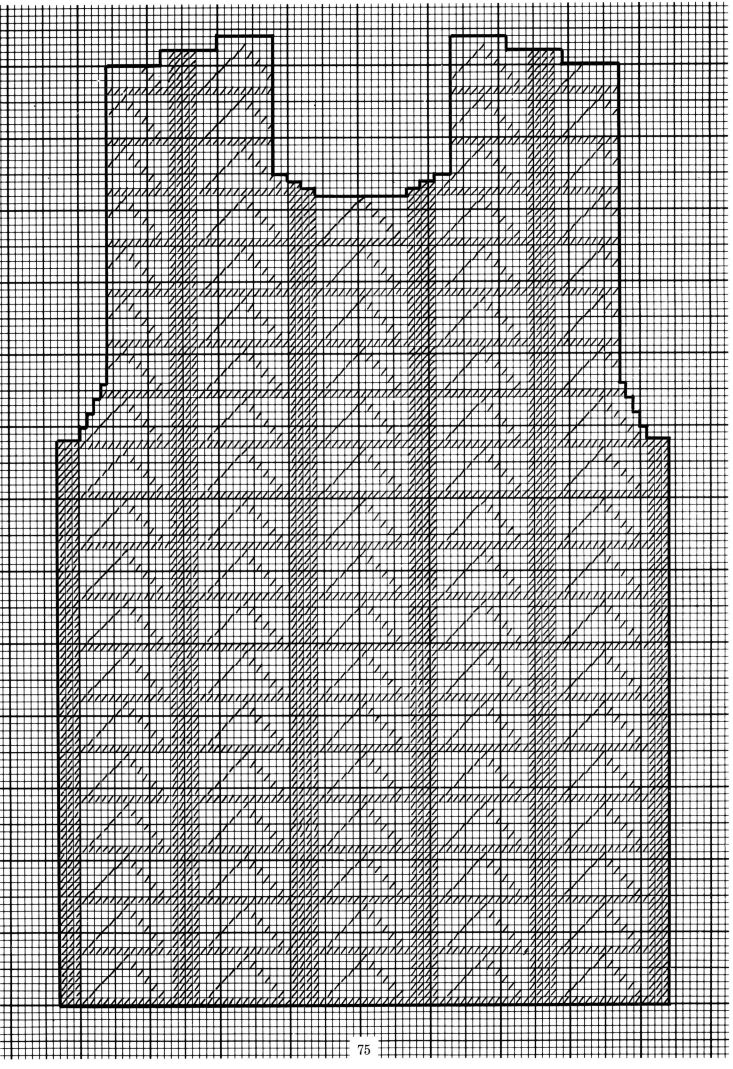

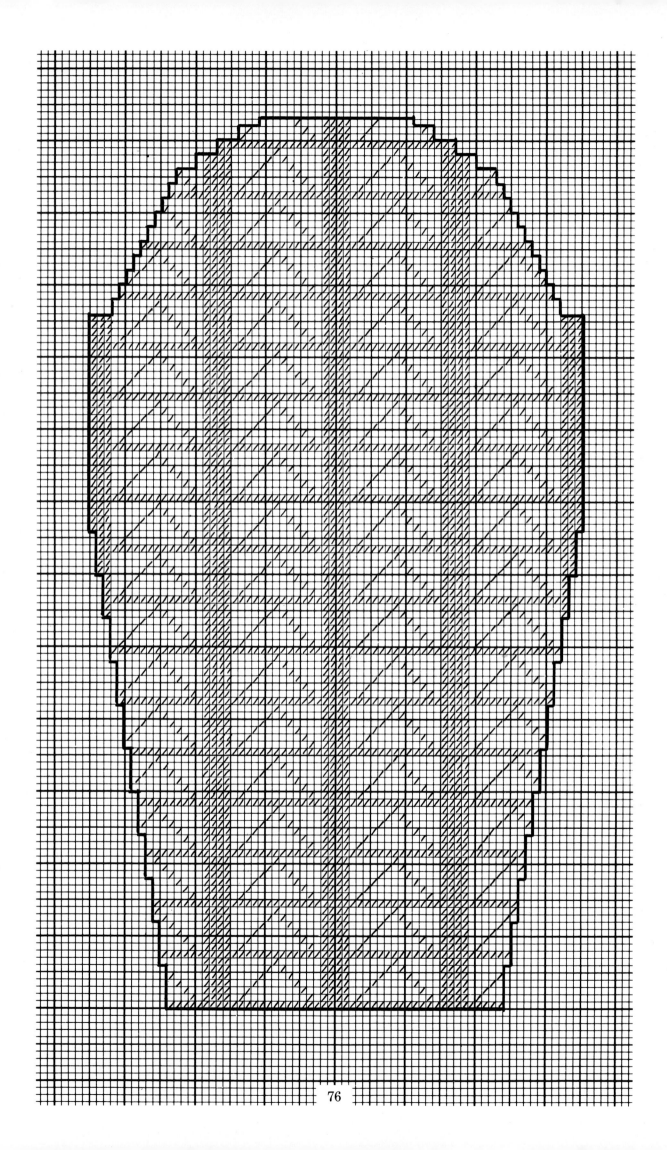

Strawberry Crew-Neck Pullover

STRAWBERRY CREW-NECK PULLOVER

Based on a popular bargello pattern of the 18th century that was used for pocketbooks and upholstery, the strawberry motif used in this pullover is a charming country design. Depending on the colors and yarns chosen, this sweater can be made suitable either for casual or more dressy wear.

MATERIALS: 16 to 18 oz. main color in sport-weight wool or cotton. 2 to 3 oz. color for strawberry. 2 oz. color for strawberry leaves. 2 to 3 oz. for squares. 2 to 3 oz. for diagonal lines.

NEEDLES: Size 2 and 5. One set of double-point needles, size 2.

GAUGE: 5½ sts = 1 inch, 6½ rows = 1 inch.

SIZE: These directions are for a size 38" finished garment. Measurements are: length to underarm 16", length to shoulder 24", length of sleeve to underarm 17".

To alter size see instructions for SIZING.

FRONT: With size 2 needles, cast on 96 sts. Work in K2, P2, ribbing for 3 inches. Change to size 5 needles and increase 12 sts evenly spaced on next row working in st st. Continue in st st and work the charted design, binding off and decreasing as indicated. Place the 28 sts in center of front on holder to be picked up later for neck ribbing.

BACK: Work back to match front. Fill in pattern at neck to shoulders and place 34 sts in center of back on holder for neck ribbing.

SLEEVES: With size 2 needles, cast on 42 sts. Work in K2, P2, ribbing for 3 inches. Change to size 5 needles and increase 8 sts evenly spaced in next row using st st. Work sleeves according to charted design.

Sew shoulder seams.

NECK: With size 2 double-point needles and right side facing, pick up and K across 34 sts on back holder, pick up and K 13 sts to front holder, K across 28 sts front holder, and pick up and K 13 sts to back. Total of 88 sts. K2, P2, in ribbing for 1 inch. Bind off loosely in ribbing.

Sew sleeves in place. Sew underarm and sleeve seams. Weave in loose threads. Block lightly with damp cloth and warm iron.

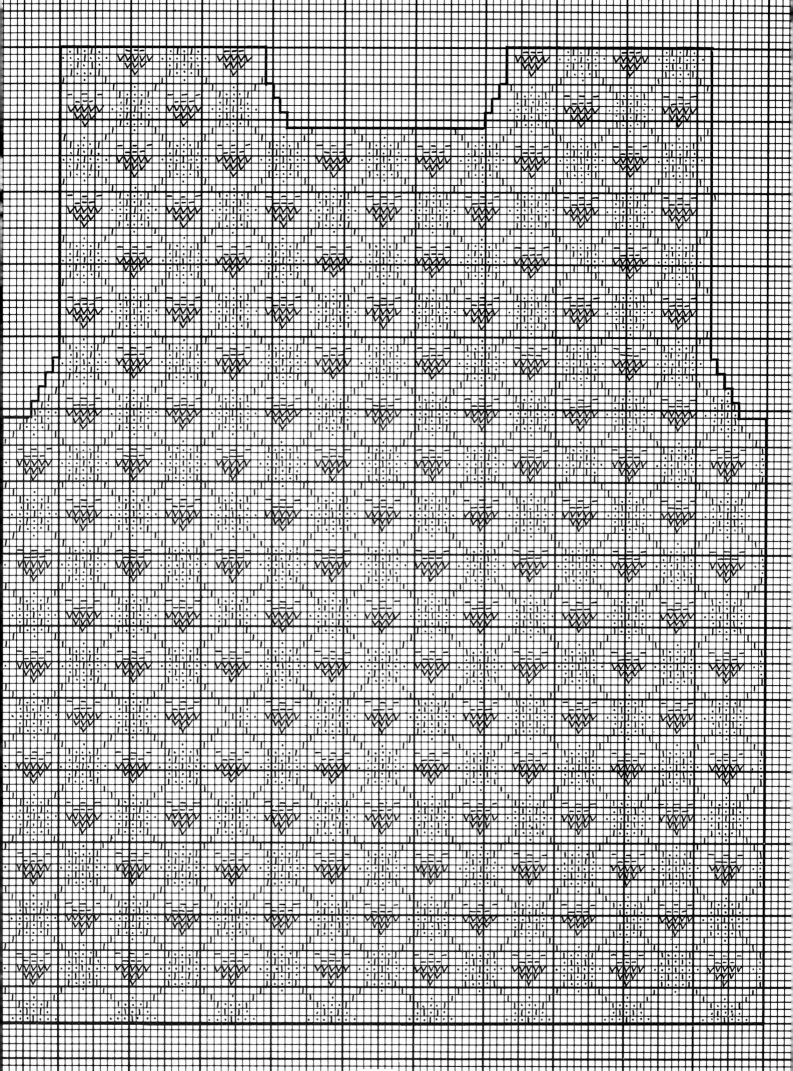

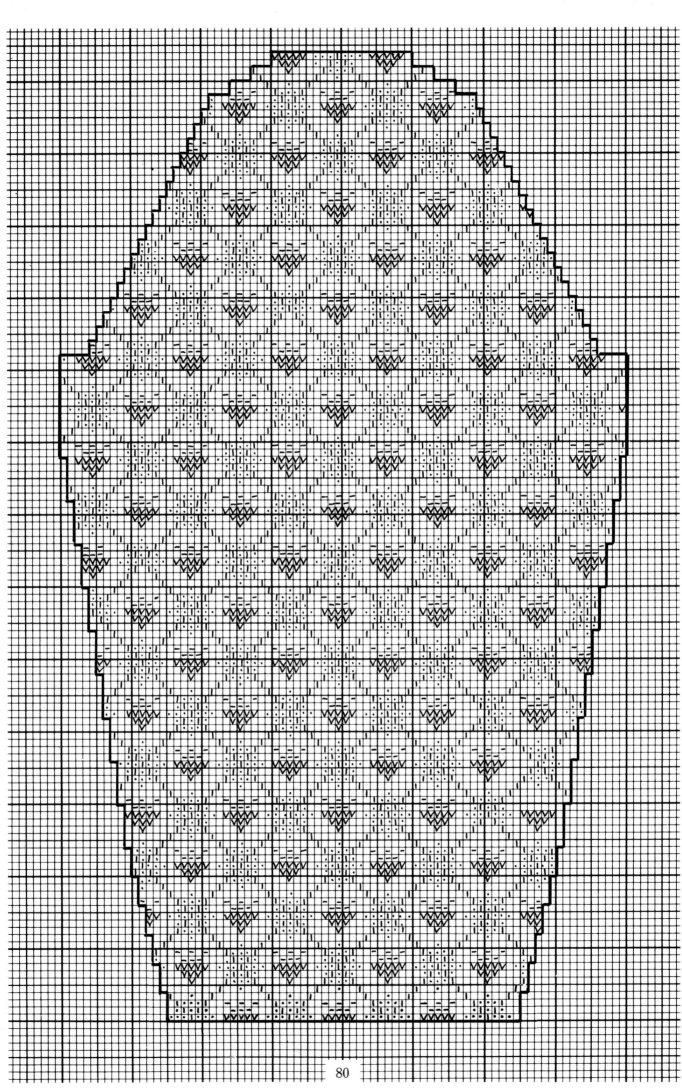

Pot of Flowers Crew-Neck Pullover

POT OF FLOWERS CREW-NECK PULLOVER

A variation on the popular Basket pattern, this sprightly design is found in innumerable versions on quilts, samplers, bed covers, and hooked rugs. As a sweater it is equally stunning and great fun to knit.

MATERIALS: 18 to 20 oz. of knitting worsted wool weight for background. 6 to 8 oz. of a contrasting color for squares. 5 oz. each of two colors for the basket. 3 oz. each of 3 colors that make up flowers and leaves.

NEEDLES: Size 4 and 7. One set of double-point needles, size 4.

GAUGE: 5 sts = 1 inch, 6½ rows = 1 inch.

SIZE: These directions are for a size 38″ finished garment. Measurements are as follows: length to underarm 15¾″, length to shoulder 25″, length of sleeve to underarm 18″.

To alter size see instructions for SIZING.

FRONT: With size 4 needles, cast on 80 sts. Work in K1, P1, ribbing for 3 inches. Change to size 7 needles and increase 8 sts evenly spaced on next row working in st st. Continue in st st and work the charted design, binding off and decreasing as indicated. Place the 14 sts in center of front on holder to be picked up later for neck ribbing.

BACK: Work back to match front. Fill in pattern at neck to shoulders and place 26 sts in center of back on holder for neck ribbing.

SLEEVES: Cast on 40 sts on size 4 needles. Work in K1, P1, ribbing for 3 inches. Change to size 7 needles and increase 8 sts evenly spaced in next row using st st. Work sleeves according to charted design.

Sew shoulder seams.

NECK: With size 4 double-point needles, K across sts on back holder with right side facing. Pick up and K 56 sts to right shoulder (including sts on front holder). K1, P1, in ribbing on 80 sts for 1 inch. Bind off loosely in ribbing.

Sew sleeves in place. Sew underarm and sleeve seams. Weave in loose threads. Block lightly with damp cloth and warm iron.

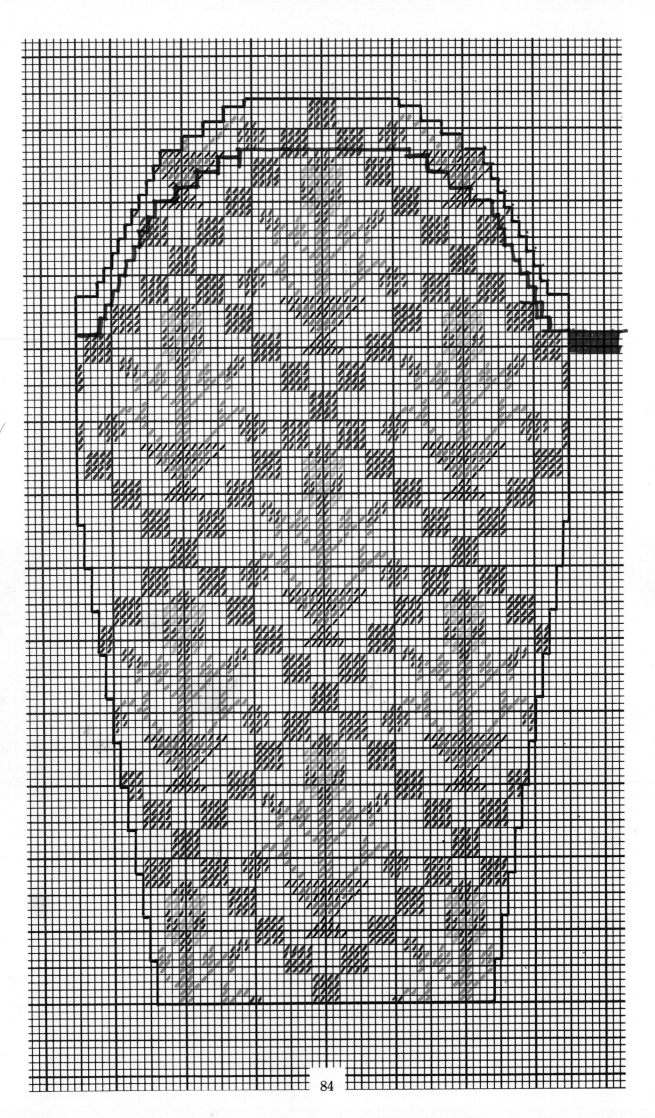

40 - 3"
add 8

Towne Border Sleeveless Vest

TOWNE BORDER SLEEVELESS VEST

Inspired by the Boston Towne Border found on woven Jacquard coverlets, this pattern combines architectural styles of the 18th and 19th centuries—center-chimney, gambrel, salt box—plus fencing and trees.

MATERIALS: 8 to 9 oz. of main color in sport-weight wool or cotton. 2 oz. of contrasting color for houses. 1 to 2 oz. of a contrasting color for outlining. 1 oz. green for trees. 1 oz. brown for trees and fencing.

NEEDLES: Size 2 and 5. One set of double-point needles, size 2.

GAUGE: 6 sts = 1 inch, 7 rows = 1 inch.

SIZE: These directions are for a size 36″ finished garment. Measurements are: length to underarm 14″, length to shoulder 21½″.

To alter size see instructions for SIZING.

FRONT: With size 2 needles, cast on 83 sts. Work in K1, P1, ribbing for 3 inches. Change to size 5 needles and increase 10 sts evenly spaced on next row working in st st. Continue in st st and work the charted design, binding off and decreasing as indicated. Place the center st on a holder to be picked up later.

BACK: Work to match front, omitting V-neck and filling in pattern to shoulders. Place 35 center sts of back on holder for neck ribbing.

Sew shoulder seams.

NECK: With size 2 double-point needles, pick up and K 35 sts from back holder, 54 sts from right front, center st of V (mark), and 54 sts from left front (right side facing). Work as follows:
Row 1: K1, P1, repeat to within 2 sts of marked st. K2 tog, P1, K2 tog, begin with P1 in ribbing across.
Row 2: Work in ribbing, dec 1 st each side of marked st.
Repeat these 2 rows 3 times.
Bind off looosely in ribbing.

ARMHOLES: With size 2 needles, pick up and K 100 sts with right side facing. Work in K1, P1, ribbing for 5 rows. Bind off loosely in ribbing.

Sew armhole and side seams. Weave in loose threads. Block lightly with damp cloth and warm iron.

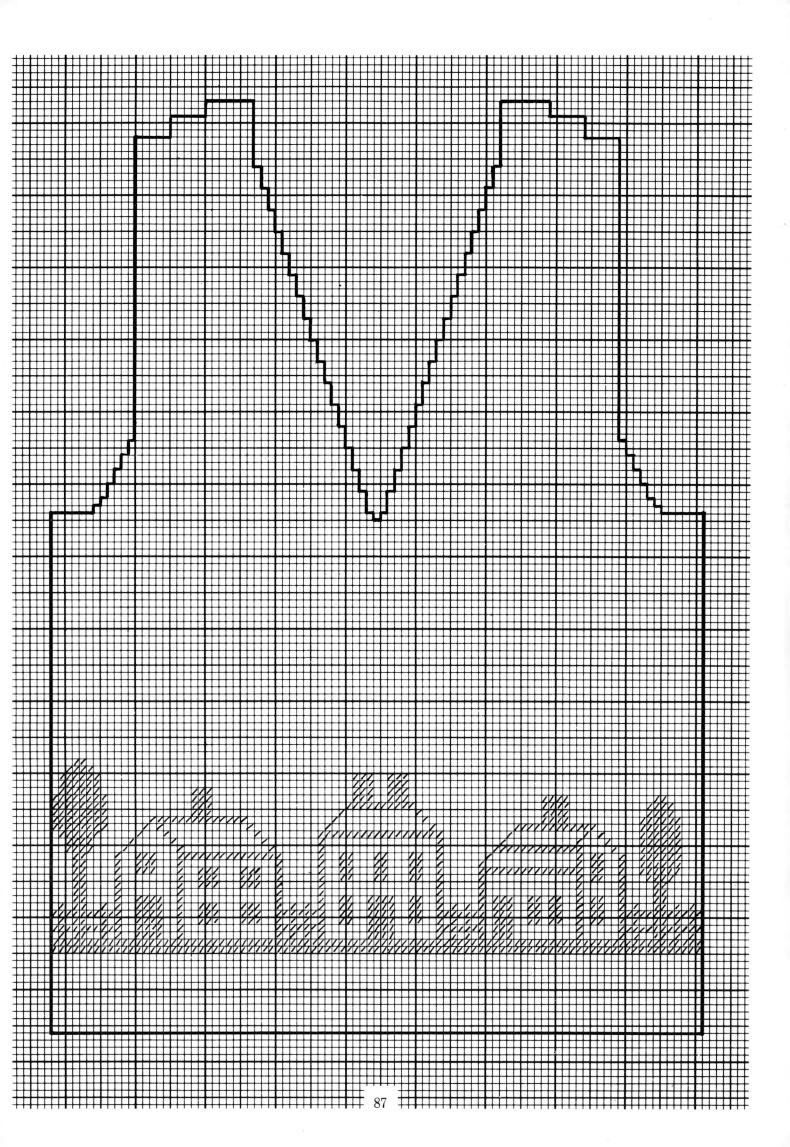

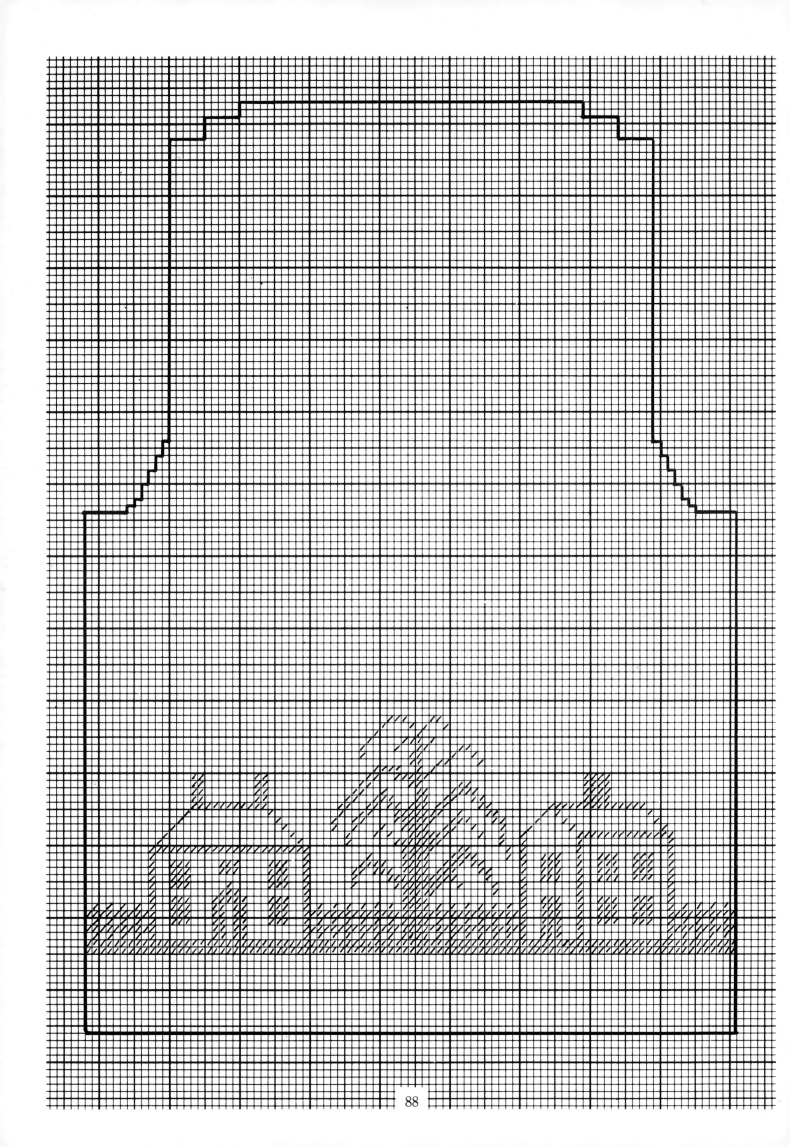

Old Rectory Crew-Neck Pullover

OLD RECTORY CREW-NECK PULLOVER

Inspired by the fascinating pattern found on the ceiling of a 12th-century English rectory, this sweater is sure to draw comments for its unique design. It is stunning, and not as difficult to knit as it might look.

MATERIALS: 12 to 14 oz. main color in sport-weight wool or cotton. 4 to 5 oz. of a contrasting color.

NEEDLES: Size 2 and 5. One set of double-point needles, size 2.

GAUGE: 5½ sts = 1 inch, 6½ rows = 1 inch.

SIZE: These directions are for a size 38″ finished garment. Measurements are as follows: length to underarm 16″, length to shoulder 24″, length of sleeve to underarm 17″.

To alter size see instructions for SIZING.

FRONT: With size 2 needles, cast on 96 sts. Work in K2, P2, ribbing for 3 inches. Change to size 5 needles and increase 12 sts evenly spaced on next row working in st st. Continue in st st and work the charted design, binding off and decreasing as indicated. Place the 28 sts in center of front on holder to be picked up later for neck ribbing.

BACK: Work back to match front. Fill in pattern at neck to shoulders and place 34 sts in center of back on holder for neck ribbing.

SLEEVES: With size 2 needles, cast on 42 sts. Work in K2, P2, ribbing for 3 inches. Change to size 5 needles and increase 8 sts evenly spaced in next row using st st. Work sleeves according to charted design.

Sew shoulder seams.

NECK: With size 2 double-point needles and right side facing, pick up and K across sts on back holder (34), pick up and K 13 sts to front holder, K across 28 sts on front holder, and pick up and K 13 sts to back. Total of 88 sts. K2, P2, in ribbing for 1 inch.

Sew sleeves in place. Sew underarm and sleeve seams. Weave in loose threads. Block lightly with damp cloth and warm iron.

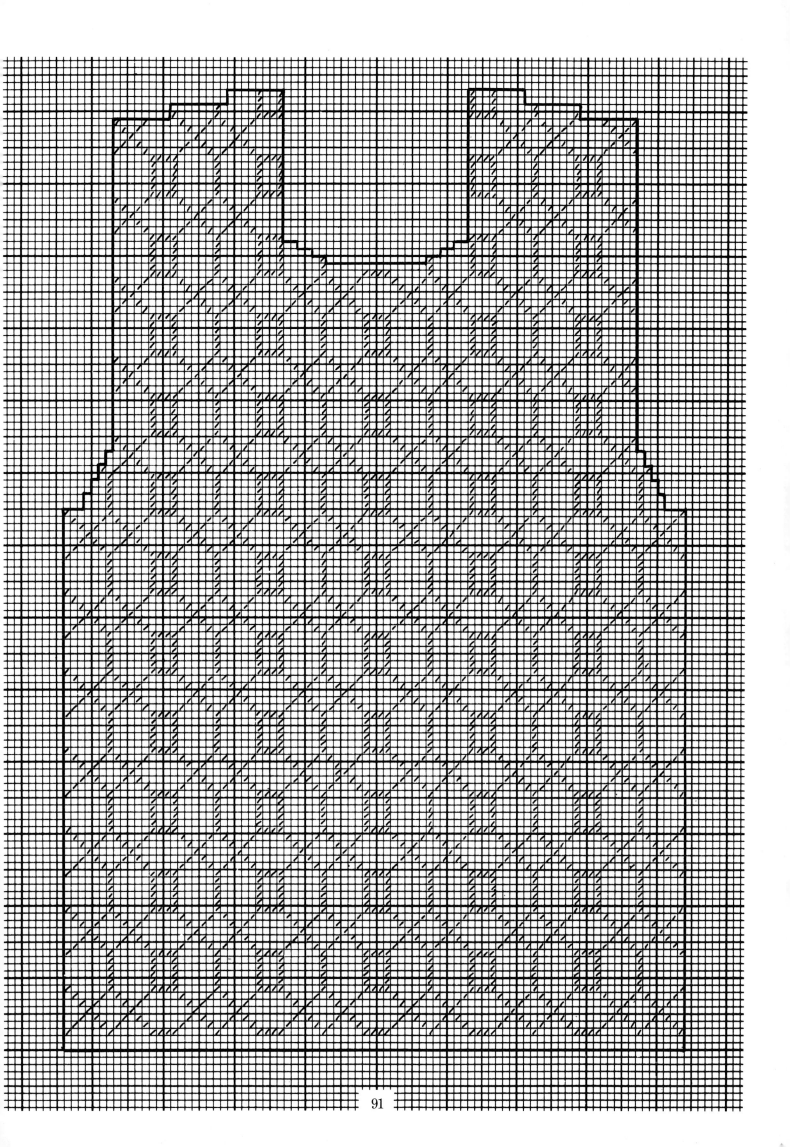

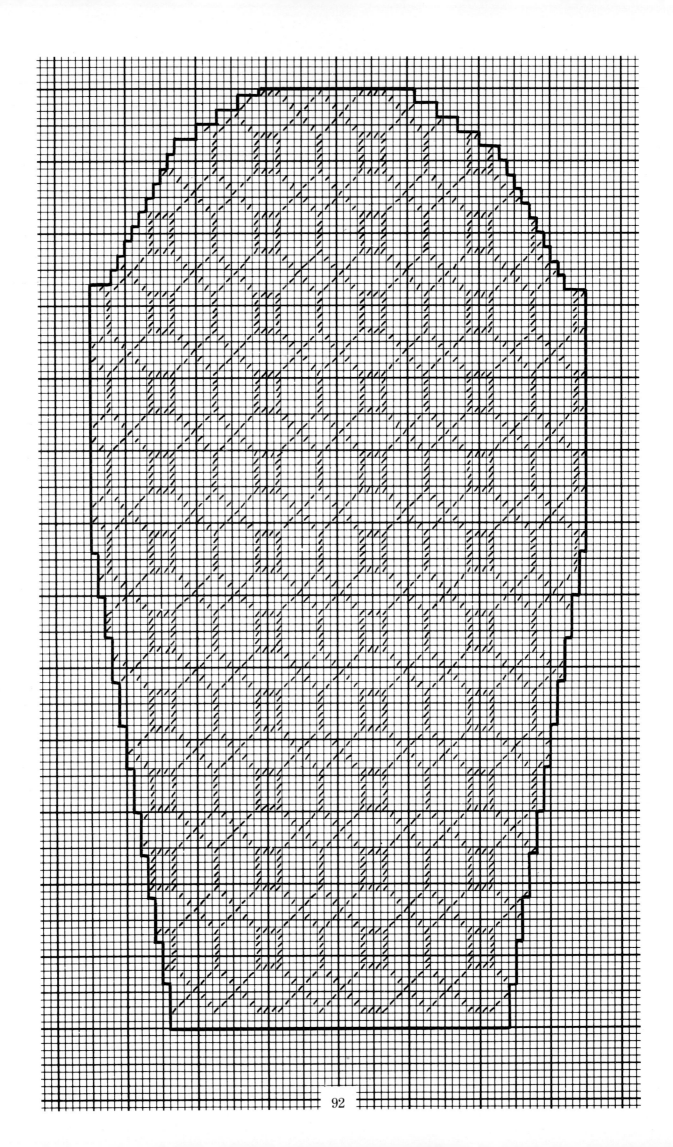

Bargello Sleeveless Vest

BARGELLO SLEEVELESS VEST

An interwoven pattern used for needlepoint in the 18th century, this adapts to a wonderful vest. Color combinations work up well either in a monochromatic scheme, or in strong contrasting colors.

MATERIALS:	4 to 5 oz. each of two colors for widest bands in sport-weight wool or cotton. 3 to 4 oz. of a contrasting color for small blocks.
NEEDLES:	Size 2 and 5. One set of double-point needles, size 2.
GAUGE:	6 sts = 1 inch, 7 rows = 1 inch.
SIZE:	These directions are for a size 36″ finished garment. Measurements are as follows: length to underarm 14″, length to shoulder 21½″.
	To alter size see instructions for SIZING.
FRONT:	With size 2 needles, cast on 83 sts. Work in K1, P1, ribbing for 3 inches. Change to size 5 needles and increase 10 sts evenly spaced on next row working in st st. Continue in st st and work the charted design, binding off and decreasing as indicated. Place the center st on a holder to be picked up later.
BACK:	Work to match front, omitting V-neck and filling in pattern to shoulders. Place 35 center sts of back on holder for neck ribbing.

Sew shoulder seams.

NECK:	With size 2 double-point needles, pick up and K 35 sts from back holder, 54 sts from right front, center st of V (mark), and 54 sts from left front (right side facing). Work as follows: *Row 1*: K1, P1, repeat to within 2 sts of marked st. K2 tog, P1, K2 tog, begin with P1 in ribbing across. *Row 2*: Work in ribbing, dec 1 st each side of marked st. Repeat last 2 rows 3 times. Bind off loosely in ribbing.
ARMHOLES:	With size 2 needles, pick up and K 100 sts with right side facing. Work in K1, P1 ribbing 5 rows. Bind off loosely in ribbing.

Sew armhole and side seams. Weave in loose threads. Block lightly with damp cloth and warm iron.

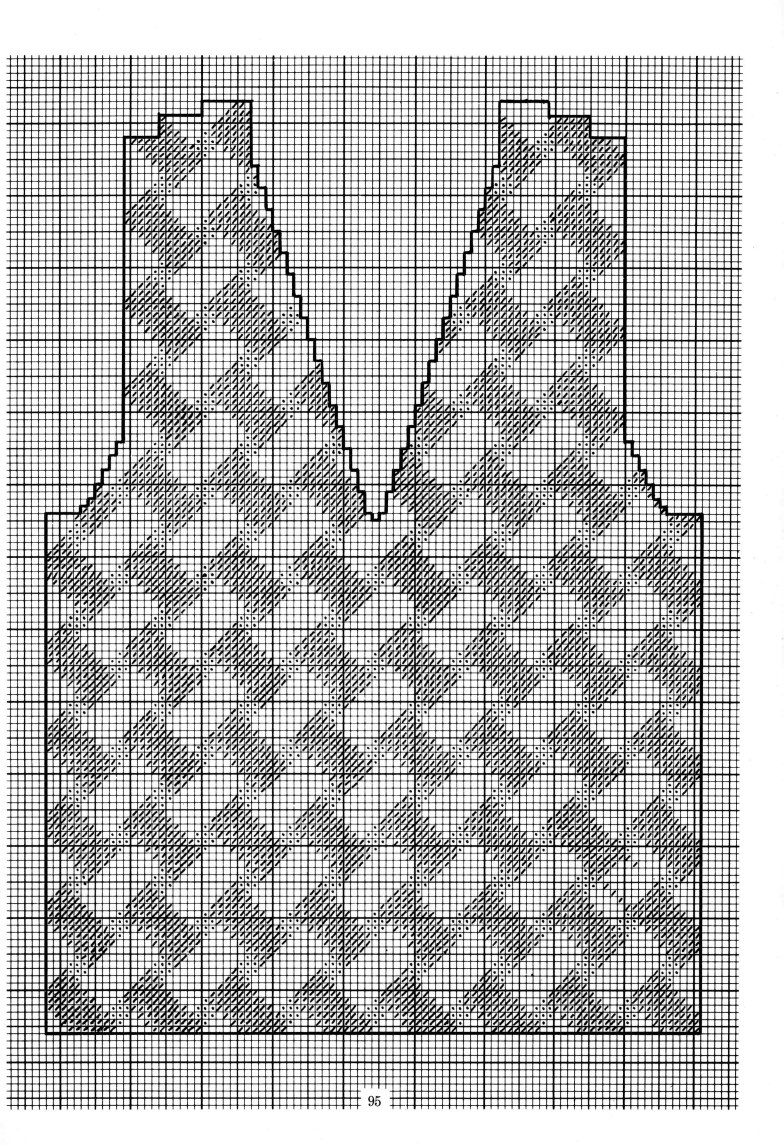

YARN MANUFACTURERS IN THE U.S.

If you have trouble finding the yarns you would like to use, contact these manufacturers for a list of the dealers nearest you.

ANDEAN YARNS
54 Industrial Way
Wilmington, Mass. 01887
(617) 657-7680
$3.00/color cards

ARMEN CORP.
(Chat Botte)
1400 Brevard Rd.
Asheville, N.C. 28806
(704) 667-9902

ARMOUR HANDCRAFTS INC.
(Bucilla)
150 Meadowland Pkwy.
Secaucus, N.J. 07094
(201) 330-9100

BERNAT YARN & CRAFT CORP.
Depot & Mendon Sts.
Uxbridge, Mass. 01569
(617) 278-2414

BOUQUET YARNS USA
51 Covert Ave.
Floral Park, N.Y. 11001
(516) 354-8537

BRUNSWICK WORSTED MILLS INC.
Brunswick Ave.
Moosup, Conn. 06354
(203) 564-2761

BUCILLA
(3 Suisses)
230 Fifth Ave.
New York, N.Y. 10021

CANDIDE YARNS
Woodbury, Conn. 06796

CASWELL SHEEP & WOOL CO.
Rt. 1, Box 135
Blanch, N.C. 27212
(919) 694-4838

CIRCULO YARNS INC.
(cotton)
7963 N.W. 14th. St.
Miami, Fla. 33126
(305) 594-0404

COLUMBIA-MINERVA
230 Fifth Ave.
New York, N.Y. 10001
(212) 685-2907

CONSHOHOCKEN COTTON CO.
Ford Bridge Rd.
Conshohocken, Pa. 19428
(215) 825-4270

CRYSTAL PALACE YARNS
3006 San Pablo Ave.
Berkeley, Calif. 94702
(415) 548-9988

DYED IN THE WOOL, LTD.
252 W. 37th St.
New York, N.Y. 10018
(212) 563-6669

E'LITE SPECIALTY YARNS INC.
750 Suffolk St.
Lowell, Mass. 01854
(617) 453-2837

ERDOL YARNS LTD.
(designer yarns)
303 5th Ave.
Room 1109
New York, N.Y. 10016
(212) 725-0162
$5/color card

FAIR DINKUM IMPORTS
7525 Harold Ave.
Golden Valley, Minn. 55427
(612) 545-6471

FANTACIA, INC.
(distributor for Lana Gatto)
415 E. Beach Ave.
Inglewood, Calif. 90302
(213) 673-7914

JOSEPH GALLER
27 West 20th St.
New York, N.Y. 10011

GRANDOR INDUSTRIES, LTD.
(Sunbeam)
4031 Knobhill Drive
Sherman Oaks, Calif. 91403

HERRSCHNERS
999 Plaza Drive
Suite 660
Schaumburg, Ill. 60195
(312) 843-6931

S. & C. HUBER, AMERICAN CLASSICS
82 Plants Dam Road
East Lyme, Conn. 06333
(203) 739-0772
$3/color card

KENDEX CORP.
(Sirdar)
31332 Via Colinas #107
Westlake Village, Calif. 91362

KIWI IMPORTS, INC.
(Perendale)
54 Industrial Way
Wilmington, Mass. 01887
(617) 657-8566
(617) 938-0077

LAINES ANNY BLATT
24770 Crestview Ct.
Farmington Hills, Mich. 48018
(313) 474-2942

LION BRAND YARN CO.
1270 Broadway
New York, N.Y. 10001
(212) 736-7937

MERINO WOOL INC.
(Emu and Picaud)
230 Fifth Ave.
20th Floor
New York, N.Y. 10001

NOMOTTA YARNS, INC.
60 E. 42nd St. #3421
New York, N.Y. 10165
(212) 687-3361
(516) 933-0994

PHILDAR
6438 Dawson Boulevard
85 North
Norcross, Ga. 30093

PHILIPS IMPORTS
(Sunbeam)
P.O. Box 146
Port St. Joe, Fla. 32456

PINGOUIN-PROMAFIL CORP.
P.O. Box 100
Highway 45
Jamestown, S.C. 29453

REYNOLDS YARN INC.
15 Oser Ave.
Hauppauge, N.Y. 11788
(516) 582-9330

SCHAFFHAUSER
938 NW Couch
Portland, Ore. 97209
(503) 222-3022

SCHEEPJESWOL USA INC.
155 Lafayette Ave.
North White Plains, N.Y. 10603
(800) 431-4040 in N.Y. (914) 997-818

SHEPHERD WOOLS INC.
917 Industry Dr.
Seattle, Wash. 98188
(206) 575-0131

SUGAR RIVER YARNS
P.O. Box 663
New Glarus, Wis. 53574

TAHKI IMPORTS LTD.
92 Kennedy St.
Hackensack, N.J. 07601
(201) 489-9505

UNTEX
21 Adley Rd.
Cambridge, Mass. 02138
(800) 343-5080
(617) 491-6744

WILLIAM UNGER
230 Fifth Ave.
New York, N.Y. 10001
(212) 532-0689

WENDY YARNS U.S.A.
P.O. Box 11672
Milwaukee, Wis. 53211

YARN MANUFACTURERS IN THE U.K. AND FRANCE

CHAT BOTTE
BP 34959056
Roubaix
Cedex 1
France

EMU WOOLS
Leeds Road
Greengates
Bradford
West Yorks
U.K.

HAYFIELD MILLS
Glusburn
Nr. Keighley
West Yorks BD20 8QP
U.K.

LISTER-LEE
George Lee & Sons Ltd.
White Oak Mills
P.O. Box 37
Wakefield
West Yorks
U.K.

PHILDAR
4 Gambrel Road
Westgate Industrial Estate
Northampton NN5 5NS
U.K.

SIRDAR LTD.
Flanshaw Lane
Alverthorpe
Wakefield WF2 9ND
U.K.

SUNBEAM
Richard Ingram & Co. Ltd.
Cranshaw Mills
Pudsey LS28 7BS
U.K.

3 SUISSES
Marlborough House
38 Welford Road
Leicester LE2 7AA
U.K.

WENDY INTERNATIONAL
P.O. Box 3
Guiseley
West Yorks
U.K.